GODS GODDESSES ~AND~ MONSTERS

A Book of World Mythology

+ SHEILA KEENAN +

ON SPELLINGS AND PRONUNCIATIONS

Most myths come from oral traditions. Their first written versions may or may not have been transcribed by indigenous people or even by writers who spoke the language natively. Therefore, there are often several ways to spell and/or pronounce mythological figure or place names. This book uses the most common English-language spellings.

ON DATES

B.C.E., Before the Common Era, is the equivalent of B.C.
C.E., in the Common Era, is the equivalent of A.D.
The abbreviation c. stands for *circa*, which means about.

PHOTO CREDITS

For my eternal hero, Kevin

Special thanks to Kate Waters for guiding this book into the real world and to Nancy Sabato for her keen designer's eye.

Thanks also to Dr. Ernest Rubinstein for his insightful comments, Belgin Wedman for her beautiful illustrations, Sarah Longacre for her excellent photo research (and Simon Taylor, Art Resource; Nancy Blum and Melissa Malnati, Bridgeman Art Library; and Christina Geiger, Christie's Images), Elizabeth LeSure for her editorial support, Barbara Balch for page design, and Christine Valentine and Susan Casel for copyediting.

Library of Congress Cataloging-in-Publication Data
Keenan, Sheila. • Gods, goddesses, and monsters / by Sheila Keenan • p. cm. • Includes bibliographical references and index. • Summary: Discusses the characters and themes of the myths of peoples from Asia to Africa to North and South America. • Mythology—Juvenile literature. [1. Mythology. 2. Folklore.] I. Title. • BL311.K44 2000 • 99-046838 • 291.1'3—dc21 • CIP • AC • ISBN 0-439-44545-0 (paperback)

10 9 8 7 6 5 4 3   03 04 05 06 07 08

Book design by Nancy Sabato • Composition by Barbara Balch • Photo research by Sarah Longacre
Map, borders, and illustrations by Belgin Wedman

Printed in the U.S.A.
First trade paperback printing, September 2003

Contents

Above: Where Do We Come From? What Are We? Where Are We Going? Paul Gauguin (1848–1903, French) was inspired by the myths and cultures of Polynesia. The title of this painting asks the same important questions mythology tries to answer.

THE WORLD OF MYTHOLOGY

If any man hopes, in anything he does, to escape the notice of the gods,
he is mistaken. —PINDAR (518–438 B.C.E., GREEK POET)

A Babylonian god slays the dragon of chaos with storm winds and arrows. Good triumphs over evil. A Jedi knight battles his dark-helmeted foe with a lightsaber and the Force. Good triumphs over evil. From ancient epics to modern movies, people have always created myths. They are one of the most fascinating and enduring forms of human expression.

People have shared myths since the beginning of time; in fact, many myths explain that very beginning. Every culture has its own wonderful stories about creation, death, gods, goddesses, or spirits, heroes, tricksters, and monsters. These myths were passed down through generations of storytellers before written language was developed. They are celebrated in art, song, poetry, and proverbs. They are reenacted in secret ceremonies or at sacred festivals. They are commemorated on every kind of structure, from temples to pyramids to totem poles.

Profound Stories

Myths are the stories people tell about what it's like to be human in a world of unseen or unknown forces. They are the answers to unanswerable questions about life and death. They celebrate good behavior and condemn evil deeds. They bring order to the cosmos by explaining the relationship between gods, humans, and the natural world. Myths are compelling, profound, and sometimes even funny.

Creation myths help explain the origin and order of the universe. Some of them start with a single, eternal creator. In others, earth and sky or the first gods emerge from a dark void or a watery chaos. Sometimes the whole universe is inside a floating cosmic egg, and life begins when the shell cracks. Animals, especially a great serpent, but sometimes even a cow, also appear in creation myths.

All kinds of myths are told about where the first humans came from: They were molded from mud or shaped on a potter's wheel. They were made out of driftwood or chopped out of a tree trunk. They formed from teardrops, sweat, spittle. Their ancestors were animals, their ancestors were gods. They once were immortal.

In many of the world's mythologies, death came about through trickery or a mistake. Myths describe death on both cosmic and personal levels. Great floods occur in many world mythologies when people annoy, anger, or ignore the gods. They wash away the world in a deluge—and a new human race begins. In certain mythologies, a whole series of worlds is created, destroyed, and recreated.

Myths about death help people face the unknown at the end of this life. Death and rebirth are eternal cycles in some mythologies.

In others, the soul leaves on a complicated journey or it lives on in an underworld of pleasure, pain, or even boredom.

The Divine, the Heroic, the Awesome

The divine beings, fearless heroes, ferocious monsters, and magical animals that inhabit mythical worlds have awed people and inspired artists for thousands of years.

At the top of many mythologies is a supreme god (although a great earth or mother goddess may once have reigned in the most ancient mythologies). Some supreme gods are mysteriously remote; others are powerful heads of an entire pantheon or family of gods and goddesses. In some very complex mythologies, there is really only one all-encompassing god; other deities are his aspects.

Ancient peoples lived very close to nature, so gods and goddesses were often linked to weather and geography. Sky deities who control the sun, wind, rain, or thunder are very prominent in world myths, as are sea gods in the myths of island and coastal peoples and fertility gods and goddesses wherever people plant crops. People worshiped these divine beings in many different ways. In some cultures, they built magnificent temples where priests and priestesses conducted elaborate rituals and sacrifices. In other cultures, natural sites were considered holy or home to the gods, and shamans communicated between the human and spirit worlds.

Most mythologies include myths about a hero and his dangerous quests and daring deeds. These myths are entertaining and instructional, because heroes are often the ones who teach people survival skills, civilized behavior, or sacred rituals.

Heroes are human, or at least half mortal— although they are bigger, braver, stronger, smarter than any living person. In mighty warrior myths, heroes defend their people against overwhelming enemies or monstrous foes. On exciting epic journeys, heroes brave all kinds of challenges to their strength and virtue. Usually they are on a mission to find a sacred object or reach a distant place, such as the underworld or the palace of the sun.

Some of the world's most popular myths are about trickster heroes. Tricksters are often wily, cunning animals. Their jokes and wicked ways get them in trouble, and their wits get them out of it. Trickster heroes help people by bringing them fire or sunlight. But in many myths, tricksters introduce death to the world.

Many myths are also full of incredible beings. Animals are worshiped as gods, honored as ancestors, or feared because of their dangerous and magical powers. Nature spirits are everywhere and must be kept happy. Monsters, giants, and serpents rage across the land or rear up out of the sea.

The Power of Myth

The power of mythology is not tied to whether its stories are logical, true, or based on historical facts. Myths are powerful because the people who share them believe in their significance. And mythology reveals a great deal about a people's religion, history, culture, social and moral codes, and their ties to nature.

Myth and religion are very tightly connected, particularly in the mythologies of living religions like Hinduism and Buddhism. Many people make distinctions between their religious beliefs and their symbolic myths. Some people do not. Other people regard all the world's sacred stories and religious figures as mythological. Scientists, scholars, and theologians continue to debate the sources and meanings of myths.

But myths are still the most popular and powerful stories ever told.

Greenland

ICELAND

North

Atlantic

Ocean

Northern Irel

IRELAN

Alaska

CANADA

PORTUG

UNITED STATES OF AMERICA

MOROCC

WESTERN
SAHARA

Pacific Ocean

Hawaiian Islands

THE BAHAMAS

MEXICO

Campeche

CUBA

HAITI

DOMINICAN
REPUBLIC

CAPE VERDE

MAUI

BELIZE

JAMAICA

Puerto Rico

ST. KITTS AND NEVIS
ANTIGUA AND BARBUDA
DOMINICA

SENEGAL

HONDURAS

GUATEMALA
EL SALVADOR

NICARAGUA

ST. LUCIA
GRENADA

BARBADOS
ST. VINCENT AND THE GRENADINES
TRINIDAD AND TOBAGO

THE GAMBIA

GUINEA–BISSAU

GUINEA

COSTA RICA

PANAMA

VENEZUELA

GUYANA

SURINAME

SIERRA LEONE

LIBERIA

Galápagos Islands

COLOMBIA

ECUADOR

French Guiana

BURKINA FASO

IVORY C

Samoa

Cook
Islands

BRAZIL

PERU

TONGA

NIUE

Tahiti

French
Polynesia

BOLIVIA

PARAGUAY

Easter Island

N

W

E

S

ARGENTINA

CHILE

URUGUAY

South

Atlantic

Ocean

Map of
WORLD
MYTHOLOGY

Some country names on this map have
been abbreviated as follows:
BEL. = Belgium
BULG. = Bulgaria
CZECH. = Czech Republic
EST. = Estonia
LAT. = Latvia
LITH. = Lithuania
LUX. = Luxembourg
NETH. = Netherlands
SLOVAK. = Slovakia
SWITZ. = Switzerland
U. A. E. = United Arab Emirates
YUG. = Yugoslavia

Myths spread as people migrate. This map

groups featured in this book. You can also see the

Ocean

RUSSIA

SWEDEN
FINLAND
EST.
LAT.
DENMARK
LITH.
RMANY
POLAND
BELARUS
CZECH
SLOVAK
UKRAINE
AUSTRIA
HUNGARY
ROMANIA
9
YUG.
BULG.
ITALY
GREECE
MALTA
CYPRUS
LEBANON
ISRAEL

KAZAKHSTAN
MONGOLIA
GEORGIA
UZBEKISTAN
KYRGYZSTAN
TURKEY
TURKMENISTAN
ARMENIA
TAJIKISTAN
N. KOREA
JAPAN
SYRIA
IRAQ
CHINA
S. KOREA
JORDAN
IRAN
AFGHANISTAN
KUWAIT
PAKISTAN
BAHRAIN
NEPAL
BHUTAN
QUATAR
U.A.E.
BANGLADESH
TAIWAN

TUNISIA
LIBYA
EGYPT
SAUDI ARABIA
OMAN
YEMEN
INDIA
BURMA (MYANMAR)
LAOS
THAILAND
VIETNAM
PHILIPPINES

Pacific Ocean

Northern Mariana Islands

Guam

FEDERATED STATES OF MICRONESIA

MARSHALL ISLANDS

NIGER
CHAD
SUDAN
ERITREA
DJIBOUTI
ETHIOPIA
SOMALIA
CAMBODIA (KAMPUCHEA)
BRUNEI
MALAYSIA
Sulawesi (Celebes)

PALAU ISLANDS

Gilbert Islands

IGERIA
CENTRAL AFRICAN REPUBLIC
CAMEROON
UGANDA
KENYA
SRI LANKA
MALDIVES
SINGAPORE
Borneo
INDONESIA

Indian Ocean

PAPUA NEW GUINEA
NAURU
KIRIBATI
Caroline Islands

DEMOCRATIC REPUBLIC OF THE CONGO
RWANDA
BURUNDI
TANZANIA
SEYCHELLES
Java
Bali
EAST TIMOR
Timor
SOLOMON ISLANDS
TUVALU

BLIC OF E CONGO
ANGOLA
ZAMBIA
MALAWI
COMÓROS

NAMIBIA
ZIMBABWE
MOZAMBIQUE
MADAGASCAR
MAURITIUS
VANUATU
FIJI

BOTSWANA
SWAZILAND
AUSTRALIA

SOUTH AFRICA
LESOTHO
NEW ZEALAND

Some small countries on this map have
been given numbers as follows:
1 Liechtenstein
2 Andorra
3 Monaco
4 San Marino
5 Slovenia
6 Croatia
7 Bosnia & Herzegovina
8 Albania
9 Moldova
10 Vatican City
11 Azerbaijan

KEY

India	Egypt	Norse Lands
China	The Near East	North America
Japan	Greece	Central America
Southeast Asia	Rome	South America
Africa	Celtic Lands	Oceania and Australia

All countries of the world, and regions mentioned in this book, are labeled.

shows the primary mythic centers of the cultural
contemporary political borders and country names.

INDIA

*In this world, there is nothing so sublime and pure
as transcendental knowledge.* —BHAGAVAD GITA

An elaborate Indian temple carving combines ancient gods and 20th-century leaders such as Mahatma Gandhi and Pandit Nehru. A cart-drawn shrine attracts urban worshipers on a street corner. A sacred cow threads its way through city traffic. India's mythology is both ancient and up-to-date, timeless and a sign of the times. It's a living mythology that is the lifeblood of its people.

Most of India's myths are part of Hinduism, one of the oldest and the third-largest religion in the world. India is also where the Buddhist and Jainist religions were founded.

The Everlasting Cycle

Unlike Buddhism, Christianity, or Islam, Hinduism does not stem from the teachings of one person. Its many layers of meaning and mythology took thousands of years to develop.

Hindu beliefs and myths are driven by two very powerful forces: creation and destruction. Everything in the cosmos, even gods and goddesses, spirals through an everlasting cycle of birth, death or dissolution, and reincarnation.

300,000,000 to One

The Hindu pantheon is incredibly complex because of the nature—and number—of its divinities. By some counts, there are 300 million *devas*, or gods and goddesses; plus all the fearsome demons, the *asuras* and *rakshas*.

Hindu gods, especially the Hindu *Trimurti*: Brahma (the creator), Vishnu (the protector), and Shiva (the destroyer); and the great goddess Devi, can appear as different forms and manifestations or avatars. Even more complicated, divine ones can be called by many, many names. Vishnu alone has more than 1,000! And because Hinduism itself is concerned with the balance of opposites such as chaos and order, its gods and goddesses also have dual natures.

There are rituals, sects, and an enormously rich body of literature, myth, and art devoted to the different Hindu deities. However, Hindus believe all these gods, in fact all of the universe, are really part of The One, The Absolute, the spiritual concept they call Brahman—who always has and always will exist.

The Path to Enlightenment

Buddhism also began in India, although its greatest impact was on the myths and religions of other Asian countries. Its founder, Prince Siddhartha Gautama, was born in northern India around 563 B.C.E. He abandoned royal life and went in search of the cause of suffering. Upon reaching enlightenment—an understanding of how to transcend the reincarnating self and reach a higher, blessed state—the prince became the Buddha. He shared the philosophical, spiritual paths he discovered with his followers, including the Noble Eightfold Path to enlightenment: right thought, right understanding, right speech, right action, right livelihood, right effort, right concentration, and right contemplation. Buddhism spread throughout India (where it was eventually absorbed by Hinduism), China, Tibet, Korea, Japan, and Southeast Asia.

Opposite: The holy city of Varanasi on the Ganges River, India

Brahma's life span is 100 years, which is how long the universe will last. But just *one* day and night, or *kalpa*, of Brahma is 8,640,000,000 human years—and there are 360 *kalpas* in a Brahma year! The Hindus use *yugas* as units to help measure this vast amount of time.

❧

Hinduism evolved from religious traditions that the Aryans, a warrior tribe, brought with them when they invaded the Indus Valley from the northwest around 1500 B.C.E. The Aryans' sacred hymns and poems, the *Vedas* (knowledge), were composed around 1000 B.C.E.; the oldest and most important was the *Rig-Veda*. Aryans believed the *Vedas* came from the breath of their divine creator. For a long time the texts were considered too holy to be written down. The *Rig-Veda* was probably not recorded until sometime in the 15th century. The Vedic pantheon included 33 gods of the earth, air, and heaven. **Indra, Agni,** and **Surya** were chief among them. **Vishnu** was a minor, benevolent deity, but he became a major figure of the Hindu *Trimurti*. The powerful Hindu god **Shiva** may also be traced back to a minor Vedic god of storms, Rudra, the "Howler."

AGNI   His bright-red skin and seven flaming tongues clearly identify this god of fire. He is at all sacrifices, licking up the butter used in the offerings. Agni, along with **Indra** and **Surya,** forms the trinity of supreme ancient gods honored in the *Rig-Veda* scriptures. His fiery powers grant immortality and also purify the sins of the dead.

ARJUNA   "Where is the joy in the killing of kinsmen?" this Pandava warrior moans in the *Bhagavad Gita*. Arjuna and his army were enmeshed in a civil war with their cousins, the Kauravas. Facing a violent, bloody battle, Arjuna was profoundly disturbed by questions about death, duty, and honor. He begged **Krishna** for help and enlightenment. The god, disguised as Arjuna's charioteer, overawed the warrior when he showed his full divine nature.

BRAHMA   He holds the *Vedas* in his four hands, and according to these sacred texts Brahma is the creator and the created. He is said to have first appeared seated on a lotus flower on **Vishnu**'s navel. He also emerged from a golden egg floating in the cosmic waters created by the divine Absolute. Brahma then created the universe. In one story, Brahma, as Purusha, the cosmic man, was sacrificed. The gods then sprang from Purusha's mouth; his head

became the sky, his eye the sun, his navel the atmosphere, and his feet the earth. In another story, Brahma as Prajapati desired his beautiful daughter. She changed into a deer to escape him, so he changed into a stag. The pursuit continued, creating all of the world's animals, right down to the ants.

BUDDHA (SIDDHARTHA GAUTAMA)   In Hindu mythology, the founder of Buddhism is considered the ninth avatar of **Vishnu.** Wondrous stories are told about his birth, and Hindu gods and demons are woven into early Buddhist myths.

DAKSHA   Born from **Brahma's** thumb, this sage did not act wisely when he invited all the gods and priests to a sacrificial feast for **Vishnu**

but left out his own daughter, Sati, and his son-in-law, **Shiva.** Shiva whirled through the feast with a host of monstrous servants. Teeth, bones, hair flew everywhere; flames engulfed the party. The angry god tore off Daksha's head (which he later replaced with a goat head).

DEVI She holds the whole universe in her womb and is considered the most powerful of the Hindu gods. Devi, also called Shakti, is many deities in one. Her different forms range from gentle and benevolent to dark and fierce. Many of the wives of **Vishnu** and **Shiva** are her manifestations. So are the warriors **Durga** and **Kali.** The great goddess was worshiped with the same devotion as the *Trimurti.*

DURGA When she rides into battle on her magnificent lion, this

▲ *In 1987, theater artists Peter Brook and Jean-Claude Carriere staged a spectacular 9-hour version of the Mahabharata. It played throughout the world. Shown here is a scene between* **Arjuna** *and* **Krishna.**

first manifestation of **Devi** is invincible. Each of her 18 arms brandishes a weapon, which she whirls furiously over her head. Her warrior skills are matched by her royal beauty. Durga was created by the energy of the *Trimurti* when all the gods were threatened by the buffalo demon Mahisha, who could only be killed by a woman. Her triumph firmly established the prominence of the great goddess.

GANESHA The goddess **Parvati** was lonely, so she wiped off some sweat and created Ganesha. She warned him not to let anyone enter and went to take a bath. Ganesha followed orders, barring even his mother's husband, **Shiva.** The outraged god cut off his head. Parvati was so upset that Shiva replaced Ganesha's head with that of the first animal he saw. That's why this god is pictured as a potbellied man with an elephant's head.

The most famous Hindu scripture is the 100,000-stanza epic, the *Mahabharata,* composed between 400 B.C.E. and 400 C.E. Glorious stories about the gods, demons, warriors, and the eternal struggle between good and evil are woven into this poem about the warring Pandava and Kaurava clans. The epic is said to have been dictated, without a single pause, by a wise man or *rishi* to the god **Ganesha,** who used a piece of his tusk to write the stanzas on a palm leaf.

One of the most revered and widely read sections of the *Mahabharata* is the 18,000-stanza *Bhagavad Gita,* or *Song of the Lord.* In this beautiful poem, **Krishna,** in answer to **Arjuna**'s questions, explains many of Hinduism's most essential truths.

❧

◄ *During the furious battle between* **Durga** *and Mahisha, the buffalo demon changed shapes, becoming a lion, a warrior, or an elephant. The mighty goddess slew each with one of her many weapons. Finally, Mahisha became a buffalo again. Durga dodged the mountains he threw at her, leaped up, and cut off the demon's head.*

CHINA

Man models himself on Earth,
The Earth models itself on Heaven,
Heaven models itself on the Way,
And the Way models itself on that which is so on its own.

—LAO ZI, *Tao Te Ching*

With their dragons, emperor gods, divine philosophers, and bureaucratic heaven and hells, Chinese myths are a fascinating blend of the fantastic and the functional.

China has the oldest existing civilization in the world. Its earliest myths date from more than 4,000 years ago, but its mythologies were ever-changing. The Three Ways: Taoism, Confucianism, and Buddhism, transformed many of the ancient stories about gods, demons, and nature.

The Three Ways

The Three Ways all began as philosophical, spiritual beliefs whose founders were human rather than divine.

Confucius (c. 551–479 B.C.E.) taught that through duty, people could achieve harmony. Order, ritual, and honoring the Five Relationships (those with parents; siblings; spouses; friends; rulers) would create a moral person and a stable society. Confucianism was a belief system that easily supported ancestor worship, family piety, and imperial power. It became the state religion in 136 B.C.E.

Lao Zi (c. 604–? B.C.E.) believed in the Tao, the essential life force of nature. Where Confucianists valued social order and good behavior, Taoists focused inward. They tried to reach a harmonious understanding of the Tao through simple living. Legend says that Lao Zi wrote his ideas in the *Tao Te Ching*, then disappeared on a water buffalo. His followers spread the master's word.

Buddhism had already been practiced in India for several centuries before it reached China in the first century C.E. The Chinese worshiped Buddha as Amitabha and practiced Mahayana Buddhism. This involved faith, repentance, and devotional acts.

Over time, popular ancient myths and legends fused with key figures of the Three Ways. Myths about Taoist and Buddhist deities and demons developed. Confucius, Lao Zi, and Buddha themselves became gods.

As on Earth, So in Heaven . . . and Hell

Earth, heaven, and hell were almost like parallel Chinese worlds. They were ruled by emperors who each headed an elaborate bureaucracy of officials and underlings. There were earthly and divine palaces, courts, and jurisdictions.

Chinese culture was an imperial culture; there was always a strong leader at the top and most emperors became gods themselves. Hierarchies are important, but so is the concept of balance. The universal opposites, yin and yang, work together to create all things and to prevent chaos. Yin, the dark, female force, is associated with Earth and the moon; yang, the light, male force, with the sky and the sun. The Taoist symbol shows them as interlocking parts of a circle—without both sides, the circle cannot hold.

Opposite: The Temple Where Prayers Are Made for the Harvest, Beijing, China

All kinds of Chinese guardians or spirits were invoked as part of everyday life. Frightening pictures of Men Shen, or door gods, were posted on doorways to prevent evil visitors from entering. Cheng Huang, or city gods, protected the land and people of each town, city, or district.

Tsao Chun, the kitchen god, was honored in every household. He was the important link between a family and the divine Jade Emperor. Every year, Tsao Chun went up to heaven and reported on each member of the household. On Chinese New Year's Eve, people smeared the mouth of his statue with honey so he would say sweet things about them.

❧

A king or emperor was considered the Son of Heaven, the person who authorized contact with the ancestor spirits and represented Shang Di, the ancient supreme god. When earthquakes, floods, droughts, and other natural disasters happened, it was a sign that the emperor of heaven was unhappy with the emperor of Earth.

DI JUN   This god of heaven and the eastern sky lived atop a giant tree just beyond the horizon. The tree was 1,000 feet wide and stood thousands of feet tall. Di Jun's children, the ten suns, hung from its branches. Each day one sun went to the treetop, was picked up in a chariot drawn by dragons, and rode through the sky. One day, all ten suns decided to dance across the sky together. Di Jun could not control his unruly suns, so he called in the great archer **Yi.**

EIGHT IMMORTALS   One had a mule that traveled thousands of miles a day—then neatly folded up into a pouch. Another shriveled up and slept in a gourd each night. They could all walk on water, float on clouds, and perform miracles to help the poor or the hungry. These popular Taoist deities were born human but achieved immortality by following the Tao, or the philosophical path. They represented different aspects of life: youth, age, wealth, poverty, or sex.

FU XI   This fish-tailed god and first legendary emperor of China was the brother of **Nu Wa.** When the thunder god destroyed Earth with a deluge, they survived by floating in a magic gourd. Fu Xi and Nu Wa married, and their children became the human race. Fu Xi taught people how to make fire and how to weave fishnets. He also shared the secrets of divination, or foretelling the future. He drew eight symbols using broken and unbroken lines. The 64 combinations of the symbols are interpreted in the famous *I Ching* (*Book of Changes*), still in use today.

GUAN DI   He was an army general before he became a god. Guan Di stood an imposing nine feet tall and had blazing eyes and a bright red face. He once killed a magistrate for molesting a girl. Soldiers then set fire to his hiding place. The general escaped, but his face was forever a fiery red. While he remained in hiding, he studied and became a Confucian scholar. Guan Di is honored as the god of war and of literature.

GUANYIN Her mercy was so great that she sacrificed her own hands and eyes to cure her father—the same father who had her killed for becoming a Buddhist nun. When her soul reached the underworld, its bright goodness shone in every dark corner, saving all the condemned. The underworld gods were so upset, they begged Buddha to send her back to Earth. Guanyin, the goddess of mercy and the bringer of children, is the female form of the Indian male bodhisattva, Avalokitesvara. She is revered almost as much as Buddha.

HUANG DI The ancient Yellow Emperor has four faces. He can look in all directions from his palace atop Mount Kunlun, the center of the world. Huang Di invented government institutions and is considered the founder of Chinese civilization. Most of his reign was a

*◀ Guanyin, the protector of pilgrims, helped **Monkey** and the Buddhist priest Tripitaka on their trip to India.*

Scientists may credit the Shang kings for founding a Chinese dynasty around 1750 B.C.E., but mythical tradition goes back much further. According to legend, before the Shang dynasty, there were Three Sovereigns (**Fu Xi**, Shennong, Yen Ti); Five Emperors (**Huang Di**, Chuan Hsiun, K'u, Yao, Shun), and the Great **Yu**, who founded the legendary Xia dynasty. There are many different myths about these rulers, who were said to have invented everything from marriage to medicine, compasses to calendars, plows to potters' wheels, agriculture to animal husbandry.

golden age. He is considered the patron god of Taoism.

JADE EMPEROR Just like the earthly Chinese emperor, this supreme god reigned over an incredibly complicated bureaucracy that mixed Buddhist and Taoist concepts. His chief assistant oversaw 75 different departments run by lesser gods. They ruled every aspect of human and animal life and tracked each individual's reincarnations.

LONG They were dragons like no others! They had camel heads and deer horns. They had tiger paws and eagle claws. And their long, reptilian bodies had 117 scales in a yin–yang balance. Chinese *long* were usually beneficial. They guarded all bodies of water, controlled the rain, and caused thunder when they rolled their magic pearls.

*◀ One of **Huang Di**'s most famous deeds was to defend his throne against the demon giant Chi You. During the battle, the giant sneezed out a thick fog. The Yellow Emperor's minister created a compass so that his army wouldn't get lost. Then Chi You flooded his enemies with a deluge of rain. Huang Di called in his daughter, Ba, whose terrific heat evaporated the waters. Huang Di finally won the battle by making a drum out of a sea monster's hide. Its terrible thunder shook mountains and paralyzed Chi You's army with fear.*

JAPAN

Though the primeval beginnings be distant and dim,
yet by the ancient teachings do we know the time
when the lands were conceived and the islands born.

—Kojiki, Preface

L ike the rising sun on its flag, Japan's
mythology celebrates two important
concepts: nature and nation. Japanese
myths honor the nature spirits of an agricultural
community and the warriors and gods of an
imperial culture.

The Way of the Gods

Most Japanese myths stem from Shinto, the
ancient religion of Japan. No one knows for sure
where this religion came from. It did not have
set beliefs, sacred books, or moral duties. Its
prayers and rituals dealt with the divine forces
of nature. For centuries, Shintoism was nameless.
It was simply called the way of the gods.

Ancient Shintoism had millions of deities,
many of them local or particular to a region.
Any natural thing that inspired awe was a *kami*,
a Shinto spirit-being. But just as Japan itself
evolved from separate clans into a more unified
country, Shintoism developed a more universal
pantheon. At the top was the sun goddess,
Amaterasu, the divine ancestor of the first
legendary emperor of Japan, Jimmu-tenno, who
was enthroned in 660 B.C.E.

Japanese Rites, Chinese Writing

Shinto myths, legends, and rituals were passed
down orally because Japan did not have a
written language until Chinese character
writing was introduced around the 5th century.
By the 8th century, the imperial rulers had
commissioned written collections to preserve
Shinto mythology, protect Japanese history,
and justify their power. In 712, the *Kojiki*
(*Record of Ancient Matters*) was recorded from
the memory of a storyteller and from several
earlier texts. This sacred work contains stories
about the origins of everything, from Earth to
the emperor.

Shintoism grew more formal. *Kami* rites and
harvest and fertility ceremonies were celebrated
in elegantly simple Shinto shrines. These
shrines were usually built of wood in beautiful
natural settings. A sacred *torii*, two tall posts
topped by curved cross beams, stood at the
shrine's entrance.

The Two Faces

Buddhism was more than 1,000 years old by
the time it traveled out of India and reached
Japan. While Shinto beliefs were very centered
in the rhythms of the natural world, Buddhism
introduced a whole new way of thinking about
life in the afterworld and reincarnation.

At the beginning of the 9th century, Shinto
and Buddhist ideas merged into a belief system
called *Ryobu*, or Shinto with two faces. Buddhist
monks held services in Shinto temples. More
elaborate Buddhist decoration was added to the
temples themselves. Shinto *kami* joined the
Buddhist pantheon as bodhisattvas. The Shinto
sun goddess Amaterasu was worshiped as a form
of Buddha.

Opposite: The Wedded Rocks, Futamigaura, Ise Bay, Japan

▶ *The 800 deities crowded around the cave entrance to trick* **Amaterasu** *out of hiding. They brought crowing roosters and set blazing fires. They hung sparkling jewels in the trees. Uzume, the goddess of mirth, made everyone laugh so loud at her erotic antics and dance that the whole earth shook. Amaterasu peered out to see what was going on. The gods said they had found a new supreme deity and held up a great mirror. The sun goddess crept out and gazed at her own reflection. A god grabbed her hand and pulled her all the way out of the cave, restoring light to the world.*

❧

The imperial ruler of Japan was thought to be descended from Amaterasu. The sun goddess blessed this sovereignty with the sacred national treasures—her mirror, her string of jewels, and the sword that Susanowo pulled out of a dragon. The mirror is in Amaterasu's Shinto-style wooden shrine in Ise. In 1946, the reigning emperor renounced his divine ancestry, but the Japanese flag still bears a bold red circle, the rising sun, symbolic of the sun goddess.

AMATERASU   The brilliant Shinto sun goddess was born when **Izanagi** washed her out of his left eye. She ruled heaven as the supreme deity but was tormented by her brother-husband **Susanowo,** the storm god. After losing a contest, Susanowo ruined his wife's rice fields and defiled her temples. Finally, he threw a flayed horse through the roof of the sacred hall where the sun goddess and her maidens were weaving divine robes. Amaterasu fled to a cave. The world plunged into deadly darkness.

EMMA-O   This god of death reigns over Jigoku, the underworld. He lives in a jewel-encrusted palace but sentences male sinners to the eight fiery or eight freezing regions of hell. His magic mirror helps him judge the dead. It reflects pictures of a person's sinful actions.

INARI   Rice is a staple of Japanese life, which makes this god of rice and husband of **Uke Mochi** a very important deity. Two red foxes act as his

messenger. Inari is sometimes considered a food goddess.

IZANAGI AND IZANAMI   The beautiful brother and sister stood on the rainbow-colored Floating Bridge of Heaven. The gods had given them a jeweled spear with which they stirred the oily ocean of chaos. A droplet fell from its point and turned into an island. The two descended and started creating the world. After giving birth to the fire god, Izanami died of a burning fever. Izanagi was crazed with grief. He followed his sister-wife to the underworld, where she told him to not to look at her while she tried to get the gods to release her. Izanagi

couldn't help himself. He lit a comb from his hair for just one glimpse of his beautiful beloved—and found her rotting corpse, pulsing with maggots. Izanagi fled, pursued by Izanami and her horde of demons, thunder gods, and devils. He barely reached the mouth of the underworld in time to close it with a boulder. Izanami threatened to kill 1,000 people every day in revenge. Izanagi then promised that 1,500 people would be born each day. From either side of the boulder, the first couple divorced, separating the worlds of the living and the dead forever.

JIZO-BOSATSU This merciful bodhisattva comforted the suffering dead, especially children who died young. The gentle monk in Buddhist robes carried a jewel that granted wishes and a ringed staff whose tinkling sound shunned darkness and evil. He could even bring souls out of hell to the Pure Land of paradise.

KANNON "The Great Compassionate One" is the equivalent of the Indian Avalokitesvara and the Chinese **Guanyin.** This popular Buddhist bodhisattva can assume any one of 33 different shapes to help answer the prayers of his worshipers.

KAPPA Their favorite foods are cucumbers . . . and blood! These vampire water spirits look like child-sized, furless monkeys. They lurk in waterways, attacking and drowning their animal and human victims, then sucking their blood. The top of a kappa's head is hollow and filled with water. If this water spills, he becomes powerless.

Zen Buddhism is one of the most important forms of Buddhism that developed in Japan. In Zen Buddhism, true insight is only possible if the mind rises above the limits of reason. Zen requires disciplined meditation and deep reflection on puzzles called koans, like the famous question, What is the sound of one hand clapping? Zen thought influenced Japanese theater, art, architecture, and even gardens. Samurai warriors adopted Zen beliefs, which helped them achieve the intuition and concentration they needed. Zen samurai inspired many Japanese hero stories and legends.

◄*After* **Izanagi and Izanami** *created an island from the swirling, jellyfish-like mass of chaos, they built a tall sacred column on it. Izanagi circled it one way, and Izanami went the other. They met face-to-face and married. Izanami then gave birth to the eight islands of Japan, the mountains, the seasons, the gods of land and water, and all the forms of nature. Izanagi created* **Amaterasu, Susanowo,** *and* **Tsuki Yomi** *when he purified himself in the sea after escaping from the underworld.*

SOUTHEAST ASIA

Impermanent are all formations.
Observe this carefully, constantly.

—BUDDHA

The geography of Southeast Asia soars up mountains and floats across islands. Its history was shaped by traders, colonists, and missionaries; waves of Hinduism, Buddhism, Islam, and Christianity absorbed its ancient religions. And from all this, a rich mythology emerged.

Southeast Asia includes the mainland countries of Vietnam, Laos, Cambodia (Kampuchea), Thailand, and Myanmar (Burma); the Malaysian peninsula; the Indonesian islands, including Sumatra, Java, Bali, Timor, and Sulawesi (Celebes); the Philippine islands; and the Malaysian-Indonesian island of Borneo.

The region was heavily influenced by the myths and religions of China and India. Magnificent Hindu and Buddhist-style temples, such as Angkor Wat in Cambodia and Borobudur in Java, rose in honor of the gods. Art forms like Bali's masked dances or Java's *wayang* shadow puppet theater developed to reenact heroic sagas, creation stories, or battles between the gods. From the 15th century on, the Muslim empire also spread. Islam and Buddhism are now the main religions in Southeast Asia.

A Layered Universe

Most Southeast Asian myth systems build on the idea of a layered universe. The basic levels are heaven, earth, and the underworld. But there are also far more elaborate myths that say there are seven layers above the earth and seven layers below. For some people, these multiple worlds represent cycles of rebirth. For others, they explain natural phenomenon. Still other cultures believe the levels are populated by different kinds of people, creatures, and spirits.

Spirits All Around

The spirit world is an important part of the everyday world in Southeast Asian cultures. Many countries trace their origins to a mythic founder, who may be a dragon or a hero or a princess married to a dragon. These ancestors are to be honored. Often they are the ones who had shown their people an essential skill, such as rice planting, cooking, weaving, or governing.

Many Southeast Asians believe that all living things came from one spirit and that things can change forms. Spirits can therefore exist in people, animals, or plants, so it is wise to honor all living things.

Villagers in much of Southeast Asia are extremely dependent upon rice crops. Cultivating the gods and goddesses of the harvest is essential. The Dayaks of Borneo make offerings to an earth spirit so he will keep the forest from encroaching on their rice fields. The Balinese hang a Rice Mother out in the field to ensure a good harvest. This guardian is made of rice sheaves. When the rice crop is later stored in the family granary, the Rice Mother is enthroned there to protect it. Thai monks intone Buddhist prayers for a prosperous rice harvest, and some Laotians even use the same word for the soul of rice and the human soul.

Opposite: Temple Borobudur, Java, Indonesia

Snakes, serpents, and dragons play an important role in Southeast Asian mythology, just as they do in China and India. There are many different kinds of underworld or underwater *nagas* (the Hindu word for snake). These creatures are part human, part serpent-dragon. The Thai god Narayana, another form of **Vishnu**, is represented by a five-headed *naga*. An enormous white serpent also is said to have defended Thailand in an ancient battle with Burma. In Malay, the Original Snake drowns people who laugh at animals, while Raja Naga, the king of marine dragons, lives deep down in the Navel of the Ocean. In Borneo, Aso protects against the forces of evil; in Sumatra, **Naga Padoha** causes earthquakes. According to legend, Cambodia was founded from the offspring of a dragon princess and an Indian Brahmin. Hanoi, the capital of Vietnam, was once called "Dragon City." Temples throughout Southeast Asia are decorated with many-headed dragons and serpents, who often guard the entrances.

ANTABOGA   Through deep meditation, this Balinese world serpent created the world turtle. A big black rock balances on the top of the world turtle's shell; two snakes coil around it. The rock covers the cave entrance to the underworld.

BATARA GURU   Indonesians and Malaysians worship the Hindu god **Shiva** under this name. The people of Sumatra believe this supreme sky god created the world while rescuing his daughter, **Boru Deak Parujar.**

BORU DEAK PARUJAR   The daughter of **Batara Guru** leaped out of heaven to escape the advances of another god. Unfortunately all that lay below was an endless ocean. Her father sent down a handful of dust, which swelled into the Southeast Asian islands. Then he scattered seeds from which sprang all animals and plants. Boru Deak Parujar married the hero who reined in **Naga Padoha,** and together they populated Sumatra with the first people.

GIMOKODAN   The dead were divided in this underworld of the Filipino Bagobo tribe. Heroic warriors slain in battle entered the red section; all others were sent to the white. There, infant spirits were nursed by a giantess covered with nipples. Everyone else existed as spirits at night but turned into dew when the sun rose.

HKUN AI   The annual Water Festival dramatically changed this Myanmar hero's home life—his

beautiful *naga* wife assumed her dragon form. Hkun Ai found this unbearable, so he left her, but first she gave him an egg. From it hatched a boy, Tung Hkam. His *naga* mother later formed a bridge so her son could cross over and marry an island princess. Tung Hkam became a powerful king.

KADAKLAN   During a storm, this god of the Tinguian mountain people in the Philippines beats his drum to produce thunder and sends out his dog, Kimat, to bite the world with lightning.

LAC LONG QUAN   This heroic dragon lord was the ancestor of the Vietnamese people. They could summon him when threatened by monsters or invaders by simply calling "Father." Lac Long Quan married Au Co, a mountain spirit. They had 100 sons, all born at once. Being a dragon, he needed to live near water, so Lac Long Quan took 50 sons to live with him in the lowlands. He taught them how to plant and cook rice and build houses. One son became Vietnam's first king. The dragon lord sent Au Co back up to the highlands with their other 50 sons. They became the ancestors of Vietnam's mountain people.

MAROMAK   The Indonesian sky god of Timor descended to Earth with the goddess Rai Lon. They created the first people, who used tree vines to pull themselves out of holes in the ground. Another Timor creation myth says that landowners came out of the hole first, followed by the common people.

MOYANG MELUR This Malaysian spirit was half man, half tiger. He lived on the moon, where he kept a hidden sack full of the rules of behavior. Meanwhile, without any laws, chaos ruled on Earth. One night Moyang Melur was watching all the murder and mayhem when he leaned out too far. He fell to Earth and threatened to kill everyone until he got back to the moon. A hunter, Moyang Kapir, lassoed the moon and they both shimmied up. Moyang Kapir grabbed the sack of rules, returned to Earth, and restored order.

NAGA PADOHA Indonesian people in Sumatra believe the underworld is ruled by this powerful, horned sea serpent. He had been pushed down into the lower depths after **Batara Guru** created the world. Naga Padoha was outraged when islands appeared in his sea. He arched his back and sent them floating away. Bataru Guru sent down a warrior to contain the serpent dragon. He pressed a huge iron weight down on the writhing creature.

NATS Offending these powerful guardian spirits of Myanmar is dangerous—they protect everything from the earth and sky to houses and villages. Nats include ghosts,

▶ *Traditional Balinese dancers in costumes and masks enact the eternal struggle between the witch **Rangda** and the spirit king Barong, who represent good and evil.*

supernatural Buddhist beings, and the most important group, the Thirty-Seven Nats. They are the souls of legendary heroes and heroines who died violently.

RANGDA Her tongue lolls obscenely to her knees. Her hair is wild, her fingernails and toenails are long, sharp claws. This Indonesian demon queen clearly represents evil. She pits her black magic against that of the good spirit king Barong. Rangda may be based on an 11th-century queen of Bali whose sorcery is said to have wiped out half her kingdom with the plague.

Sky gods and birds are often creators in Southeast Asian myths. In Indonesia, Lowalangi, god of the sky and winds, breathes souls into human beings. In Borneo, Tingang, the rhinoceros bird, made the world tree from which all people descended. The Dayak people of Borneo say that two bird spirits, Ara and Irik, formed the first people from dirt; they came to life when they heard the birds' calls.

AFRICA

A river is filled by its tributaries.

—PROVERB

frica. Its deserts, forests, and savannahs cover 20 percent of the earth's land. Its many peoples speak more than 1,000 languages. And its mythologies are just as vast and varied.

Migration and Colonization

Africa did not develop one overall myth system because Africa itself does not have one people, one history. What it does have is a complex heritage of many different tribal groups. Some were nomadic, some established great kingdoms, and some migrated throughout the continent, influencing local culture and beliefs.

The continent was also heavily colonized by Europeans, Arabs, and Asians, who established many African nations' modern borders. They also brought with them Islam and Christianity, which often dominated or destroyed the local African deities. Because of this history, there's no easy way to group the mythologies of Africa. The broadest category is geographic: West Africa (Nigeria, Benin, Ghana, Mali, and neighbors); East Africa (from Sudan down to Mozambique); and central and southern Africa (Cameroon, Congo, The Democratic Republic of Congo (Zaire), Zimbabwe, South African Republic, and most countries in between).

Spoken Myths

African myths were shared through ritual storytelling, proverbs, chanted poems, or songs. Most of Africa had no written language, so myths were not really recorded until the 19th century and were influenced by the ideas of the European Christians who wrote them down.

Serpents, Spirits, and Supreme Gods

Many African mythologies include a supreme god who created and peopled the world. A world serpent often helped him or was a force of creation itself.

In many cosmic myths, human beings were originally immortal and lived in close harmony with the creator god. They lost both of these privileges: Divine messages gone awry often introduced death; disrespectful human behavior often alienated the supreme god.

But if the supreme god was aloof, African spirits were alive! Ancestor and nature spirits were very important to most African groups. *Ngangas*, or shamans, were the go-betweens of the human and spirit worlds. Through sacred rituals, they could contact the ancestors, heal the sick, and prophesize through divination.

Twins and Tricksters

Many, many African creation myths involve twins. Twins symbolize the dual nature of the world, like light and dark or good and evil. They can be distinct figures: male, female; the sun, the moon; day, night; or a male–female deity. Twins signify balance in most stories. Tricksters, on the other hand, are anything but balanced figures. Mischievous gods or animals, they delight in upsetting order or outwitting others. Stories about animal tricksters are particularly popular African myths.

Opposite: A Dogon village on the Bandiagara Cliffs in Mali

Death was not always a given. In the beginning, most African creator gods did not include death in their work. That came later, usually because of a mistake or a garbled message. The Zulu supreme god, Unkulunkulu, sent a chameleon with news of eternal life. He sent a lizard with that of death. The swift lizard outstripped the slow-moving chameleon. In a Baluba myth, an old grandmother asks to be left alone while she performs a secret ceremony of immortality. She's interrupted shedding her skin and dies. According to the Nuer, a rope once dangled from heaven. Old people climbed it, were rejuvenated, and returned to Earth. A wicked hyena cut the rope.

*▶ Nommo, divine offspring of **Amma** were ideally balanced twin creations. The Nommo helped create life on Earth, day and night, and the seasons. The Dogon honor them for sending a blacksmith who floated down on a rainbow in an ark filled with plants, animals, minerals, a spark of fire, and the ideas that became human society. This Dogon stool shows two Nommo with upraised arms.*

AMMA A great egg shook seven times, split, and this supreme god came forth. Amma made the sun and the moon from clay pots. He also molded the earth from clay and mated with her. A beastly jackal was born. Then Earth bore the twin creator deities, the Nommo. After Amma created the first man and woman, they also bore twins, four boys and four girls, the ancestors of the Dogon people of Mali.

ANANSE He saddled tigers and beguiled snakes. He snatched a fishing song from the water spirits and bargained for the stories of the sky god **Nyame**. The Ashanti people of Ghana tell many popular trickster tales about this spider who could outwit animals, people, and

even gods. Ananse has an uncanny ability to figure out what others are thinking—and uses cunning to turn this into his own good fortune. In some myths, Ananse also helped with the creation of the sun, moon, stars, and human beings.

CHUKU The Great Spirit of the Ibo in Nigeria sent a dog to tell people to cover a dead body with ashes, and it would return to life. But the dog got tired and stopped to rest. Next, Chuku sent a sheep with his message. But the sheep was hungry and stopped to eat. Then it muddled the message and told people to bury their dead. The dog arrived with the right words too late. Humans had lost the chance to become immortal.

ESHU This Yoruba trickster god is a messenger—and a meddler. Speaking all languages, he brings messages from the gods to people, and sacrifices from people to the gods. He also stirs up fights and quarrels with the tricks he plays on kings, commoners, and even other gods. The Fon people of West Africa know him as Legba.

GU It is fitting that this heavenly blacksmith was born as a stone with a sharp cutting edge. The Fon of West Africa believe that on the second day of creation, Gu was sent down to Earth by his parent **Mawu-Lisa** to help their ancestors survive. He taught them how to clothe, feed, and shelter themselves. He also gave them the precious knowledge of toolmaking and metalworking.

HARE This wily and often lazy animal appears in many African trickster myths. In one, he tricks an elephant and a hippopotamus into a tug of war. Their pushing and pulling clears Hare's fields for planting. In another, he outwits an antelope and a lizard so he can eat their crops and drink from the lion king's water hole, which they guarded. Crafty though he is, Hare is often outwitted by **Tortoise.** According to a Khoi (Hottentot) myth, Hare has a split nose because Moon hit him with a stick after he gave people the wrong message about immortality.

JUOK People are different colors, the Shilluk of the Sudan say, because Juok made them from different soils. He used white, reddish-brown, and black clays to create human figures. Then he gave them long legs like flamingos so they could run, long arms like monkeys so they could swing hoes, mouths to eat and sing, eyes to see food, and ears to hear their own songs.

KAANG The creator god of the San (Bushmen of the Kalahari) is a resurrecting god. When an ogre enemy eats him, Kaang is vomited back up; when he's killed and devoured by ants, his bones shake

▲ *African stories about Hare and other animals traveled to the United States with enslaved peoples. They were transformed into folktales about Brer Rabbit, Brer Bear, and others. Joel Chandler Harris (1848–1908) collected these oral stories in his famous Uncle Remus books.*

back into a skeleton. He formed the moon out of an old shoe, created the first humans, but then retired to an unknown place in the sky when people disrespected him.

KHONVUM Every night this creator god of the Pygmies fills a sack with broken pieces of the stars. He tosses them at the sky so that the sun will rise again in the morning. A great hunter, his serpent bow is the rainbow, and he talks to his subjects through animals, often a chameleon.

There are many African myths about the first people. A Zaire myth says the first being was actually a palm tree with a male head and a female head; the tree later split into the first humans. A Gabonese story tells about Fam, the immortal first man, who was created to rule above even the mightiest animals. But Fam disrespected the creator god and was banished below the earth. According to the Fon, Adanhu and Yewa, the first man and woman, stayed on Earth only long enough to teach their children the ways of the gods, then they returned to heaven. The Bakuba believe that the creator god Mbombo vomited out the first man and woman; the Ashanti believe a python helped the first woman conceive the human race; and the Pangwe of Cameroon say that God molded a tailless clay lizard, left it in water for seven days, and then commanded, "Man, come out!"

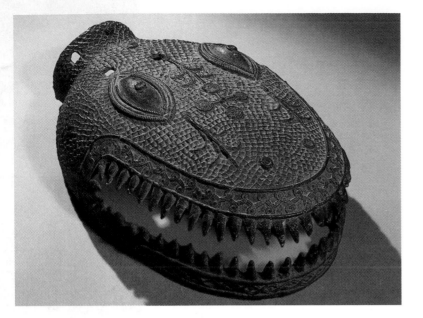

▲ Cosmic serpents and snakes, especially pythons, appear in many African myths. They can be part of the primal forces of nature, carry messages from ancestors or spirits, or help with medicine or childbirth. This beautiful metalwork snake head is from Benin.

Dan Ayido Hwedo, born of **Mawu-Lisa**, is a rainbow serpent whose male sections are red and female sections blue. With its tail in its mouth, this serpent encircles and supports Earth with thousands of coils. The movement of this great python keeps the cosmos in motion but also can cause earthquakes.

KINTU   When he came to Uganda, he had nothing but a cow. All he drank was milk, all he ate was cheese. Nambi, daughter of the sky god Gulu, fell in love with this first man, but her father forbade the marriage until Kintu performed several formidable tasks. First he was ordered to eat a huge meal of thousands of bananas, plates of meat, and gourds of beer. Kintu buried the food in a hole in the floor. Then he had to fill a pitcher with only dew water. He set it in a field until it filled itself. Finally, he had to pick out his own cow from a huge herd of 20,000. A sympathetic bee landed on the horns of Kintu's cow so he could find it. Nambi and Kintu married and headed back to Earth with the cow, a goat, sheep, chicken, and a banana plant. Gulu told them not to turn back, no matter what. However, the couple forgot the chicken feed and returned to heaven to get it. There, Nambi's brother insisted on traveling to Earth with them. His name was Walumbe—or Death.

LEZA   A sky god worshiped by Bantu speakers in central and southern Africa, he gave a bird three calabash gourds to bring down to people; two held seeds and the third was to remain sealed. Like the Greeks' **Pandora,** the bird was too curious. When he opened the third calabash, danger, death, and disease were loosed upon the world.

MAWU-LISA   Mawu is the female spirit of the night, the moon who lives in the west. Lisa is the male spirit of the day, the sun who lives in the east. These creator deities could be twins or a double-sexed deity, but together they represent universal balance and order. From them came all of the vodu, or gods, of the Fon people of Benin. Mawu-Lisa had seven sets of twins who became sky gods, thunder gods, earth gods, and sea gods. **Gu,** Legba, and Dan, one of whose forms is the divine serpent Dan Ayido Hwedo, are among their children.

MODJADJI   She lived in the misty Drakensberg Mountains in the Transvaal of South Africa. The Lovedue worshiped and sacrificed to this goddess so she would send rain clouds to water their crops and use her fierce magic to wither their enemies.

MWAMBA AND SELA   When the creator god **Wele** made this first man and woman, he settled them into a house on stilts just like the heavenly house he'd built for himself. The couple was careful to guard the entry ladder to their house to prevent monsters from ascending. Their children eventually climbed down and populated the earth.

MWUETSI The creator god of the Makoni (Zimbabwe) made this first moon man, gave him a horn full of magic oil, and sent him to live at the bottom of a lake. Mwuetsi ignored God's warnings and moved up to the land. He wailed when he saw how barren it was. God took pity on

Mwuetsi and sent him a female companion. The moon man used his magic oil, and the morning star maiden gave birth to the trees and fruits of the earth. After a few years, she returned to the lake. Mwuetsi mourned so much that God sent him the evening star maiden. They coupled, and she bore farm animals and humans. Despite another sign from God, the two still coupled. The evening star now bore wild animals and a huge mamba snake. She warned Mwuetsi not to approach her bed anymore, but eventually he did. The huge snake uncoiled from beneath the bed and bit Mwuetsi. He became so sick that the rains dried up, plants and animals died, and his own children strangled him and threw him back in the lake.

NYAME Great and Shining One. Giver of Rain. Creator Architect. The Ashanti of Ghana had many names for their supreme god. Nyame is a benevolent god who was worshiped in the form of a tree trunk. The Ashanti sent their prayers or complaints through the god's go-between, **Ananse.** Spider helped Nyame during the creation of the world and humankind. Because of him, Nyame saw the need to create day and night, so people could work and rest; the sun and moon to heat the day and illuminate the night; and wind and rain for balance. Nyame united the Ashanti people under one king by sending a golden stool floating down from heaven. It contains the soul of the nation, and no one is allowed to sit on it.

Animals play significant roles in African myths, and they're often given human characteristics. The elephant is considered a wise, fair judge; the leopard is a symbol of royalty, and its hide is used only by kings. Lions are sometimes seen as manifestations of a god or reincarnations of kings and queens, while the mischievous, evil jackal is the child of the Dogon god **Amma.** The praying mantis is often identified with the San (Bushmen of the Kalahari) god **Kaang;** the San also credit the insect with bringing them fire. Other fire-bringers include a wasp (Ila) and a dog (Nile River peoples)

❧

◄ *Masks are often used in African rituals as powerful symbols of a god or spirit. Shamans, usually male, enact the traditional ceremonies. Music, dance, and costumes are often included. The form and beauty of African masks have inspired artists from Picasso to the designers of the Broadway play, The Lion King. This "mask of authority" comes from the Kuba tribe, Congo. It represents their heroic ancestor, Woot.*

Obatala was also called Orishnala. He wore long white robes and lived in a gleaming white house. One day his jealous servant sent a huge boulder hurtling down onto Orishnala's house. The god was crushed, and divine pieces of him flew everywhere. **Orunmila** quickly scooped up as many pieces as he could, but the result was the creation of 401 *orishas*, Yoruba deities. The Yoruba, as well as the Fon and the Ashanti, have maintained their strong religious traditions.

❧

Vodun (or Voodoo), the main religion of the Caribbean island of Haiti, can be traced back to West Africa. West Africans who were enslaved and transported to the island brought their religious traditions and myths with them. Divinities like Legba (**Eshu**) number among the *loa* or Vodun gods and spirits. Haitian Vodun has also been heavily influenced by Christianity.

❧

▶ *Olukun had mudfish legs and a lizard staff. He lived beneath the sea in a palace decorated with all the riches on Earth. Yoruba women in Benin and Nigeria prayed to him for children, sailors for good luck in their seafaring.*

OBATALA   His divine father, **Olurun,** gave this Yoruba god a snail shell full of earth and a chicken and sent him down to create the world upon the primeval waters. Obatala sprinkled the earth, and the chicken spread it by scratching. Land formed everywhere. Then the god sculpted 16 forms out of mud, and Olurun gave them life. They became the great gods and clan ancestors of the Yoruba people.

ODUDUWA   Sometimes she is portrayed as the primeval earth, the mother of all Yoruba, and the wife

or sister of **Obatala.** In other myths Oduduwa is a male god, a warrior, and the first Yoruban king. This deity is said to have finished the act of creating the world after Obatala got drunk on palm wine and fell asleep. **Ogun** and **Shango** are among Oduduwa's offspring.

OGUN   The earth was originally heavily forested, but this Yoruba god forged an ax and bushwhacked a way through so the gods could descend and people could plant. A skilled metalworker, a zealous hunter, and a fierce warrior, he is the god of iron and of war. Soldiers, taxi and truck drivers, and all who work with metal tools worship Ogun and offer sacrifices for his blessings.

OLUKUN   Before the sky god **Olurun** created the universe, only he and Olukun, the primeval waters, existed. The water god challenged Olurun's supremacy. Since Olukun loved beauty and wealth, he suggested a contest to see who could display the finest robes. Olurun appeared as an ever-changing chameleon and bested Olukun's every outfit. Some myths say these gods together gave birth to **Obatala** and **Oduduwa.**

OLURUN   Owner of Heaven. Owner of Life. Owner of the Day. Just a few of his names indicate the supreme position of this sky god. He heads a Yoruba pantheon of 1,700 deities. Olurun created everything from night and day to destiny and death. He's also called Olodumare.

ORUNMILA Also called Ifa, this is the Yoruba god of divination. He is the adviser to **Olurun** and translates that supreme god's messages back to his worshipers. Orunmila once lived on Earth, where he taught people the healing arts. After being insulted by his children, he returned to heaven. They begged him to come back, but instead he gave them six palm nuts, or *ikin*, to be used for prophecy. Yoruba priests perform the Ifa divination rituals by shaking and interpreting the combinations of the nuts.

SHANGO He breathes fire and wields a magic thunderbolt. He was a divine Yoruba king who vanquished his foes and foiled his own disgruntled, war-weary people by vanishing into the forest. Shango ascended to heaven and is worshiped as the Yoruba god of thunder and lightning. He is often shown with a double ax on his head, the symbol of thunder.

TORTOISE A lion once grabbed this animal, ready to eat him. Clever Tortoise told the lion to put him in water to soften his shell first. The lion did—and Tortoise swam away. He also caused the first sunrise by rescuing the sun, imprisoned in a cave. Tortoise grabbed the orb in his claws, and a bird friend lifted them both into the sky. Steady and wise, this animal is featured in many African tales, sometimes with **Hare.**

WELE This creator of the Abaluyia of Kenya made the universe in six days—including settling a spat between the sun and the moon. The moon shoved the sun out of the sky; the sun threw the moon down to Earth and splattered mud on him. Wele created night and day to separate them. He then went on to create everything in the sky and on Earth, including **Mwamba and Sela.**

African spirits abound, from the savannah to the swamp. Ancestor, animal, or other spirits could dwell in a fetish. The fetish would protect its owner against harm. Fetishes could also be used by sorcerers for evil purposes. Other spirits include *kishi*, an evil, people-eating spirit with two faces, one human, one that of a hyena. *Tebos* are ugly dwarfs who snatch victims and eat them; while *li* invade a victim's intestines and also eat corpses. On the other side, the good *malaika* is an angel-like spirit who protects people, as do *bakulu*, or ancestor spirits.

∾

◄ *This pre-19th century fetish from Zaire, served as a container for the spirits of the dead.*

EGYPT

Every heart swelleth with joy at thy rising forever.

—Hymn to Ra, the Sun God, *The Book of the Dead*

Egypt. The Nile. It's almost impossible to say one without thinking of the other. Along the banks of the world's longest river the Egyptians created one of the most sophisticated and monumental of ancient civilizations.

Life, Death, and Crocodiles

Ancient Egypt was a country where nature could be extreme. Lush riverbanks bordered arid desert sands. Most Egyptians depended upon agriculture, a continual cycle of sowing and reaping. The hot sun could be withering or beneficial to their crops. The Nile was life-giving during its annual flood or deadly during a drought. Dangerous animals like jackals and lions roamed its shores; snakes, crocodiles, and hippos lurked in its waters. There was no escaping the dual forces of the natural world or the universal opposites, life and death.

This played an important role in Egyptian mythology. The sun was worshiped as the supreme god; water was the mythic source of chaos and creation. Gods and goddesses were often shown as humans with animal heads. The animal's attributes symbolized the deity's power.

Divine Royalty

Ancient Egypt did not have one universal pantheon. In fact, ancient Egypt was not even one country, it was 42 tribal areas, or *nomes*, each ruled by a chieftain. The nomes had their own gods and goddesses. Mythologies blended as the nomes consolidated, because Egyptians did not discard gods, they rearranged them. Sometime between 3500 and 3100 B.C.E., Egypt united as one country, under one ruler—the divine pharaoh.

According to myth, the gods themselves were the first kings of Egypt. When they tired of that role, the pharaohs took over. The pharaoh was human but was considered divine. He was called the son of Ra, the sun god. He represented Horus, the sky god. When the pharaoh died, he became Osiris.

Life in the Afterlife

The most profound aspect of Egyptian life was its cult of death. Egyptians prepared for an afterlife that would be similar to their present life. Embalmers preserved dead bodies with special chemicals and linen wrappings in a process called mummification. This was supposed to make the body everlasting so that it could later reunite with the dead person's spirit soul.

Mummies were placed in beautifully decorated cases and then buried in tombs, along with everything from jewelry and cosmetics to food, crockery, and *shabtis*, or carved figures of servants who could do your work for you in the next life. Royal tombs were hidden deep inside the pyramids or in temples carved into cliffs. They were filled with ornate burial items, many of them made of gold. Tomb paintings or the papyrus *Book of the Dead* were included to provide the dead with prayers and spells for navigating their way through the underworld.

Opposite: The Sphinx and Great Pyramids at Giza, Cairo, Egypt

THE NEAR EAST

He saw the great Mystery. He knew the Hidden.

—Tablet 1, *Gilgamesh*

Civilization started here—and with it came influential gods, goddesses, heroes, demons, and mythical beasts. The ancient Near East produced deities later found in Greco-Roman mythology, like dying and rising gods and powerful fertility goddesses. Ancient Mesopotamian or Persian accounts of the great flood, a garden of paradise, and the fires of hell predate those in the Bible or the Koran.

A Civilized World

The world's first civilizations arose in Mesopotamia, which is now Iraq. People had been living in the Near East for thousands of years, but around 3500 B.C.E., the Sumerians became the first to build cities in the fertile lands between the Tigris and Euphrates Rivers.

Invade and conquer was the rule in the ancient Near East, which meant civilizations were forever expanding and contracting. In Mesopotamia, the Akkadians, Assyrians, and Bablyonians, among others, followed the Sumerians. Each culture absorbed much of the rich mythological traditions of the Sumerians. Other ancient peoples with their own mythic ideas also inhabited the Near East, often overrunning their neighbors. The Canaanites, including the famous seafaring Phoenicians, lived in what is now Syria, Israel, Lebanon, and Jordan. In Anatolia (central Turkey), the Hittites with their horses and chariots were mighty empire builders. By the 6th century B.C.E., Persia (Iran) had created the largest empire in the ancient world.

Living Myths

As in most ancient cultures, Near Eastern myth, religion, and government were inseparable. Kingship was a divine gift, although the king himself was not divine. The gods, who usually had human forms, lived in their high ziggurat temples and owned the cities below. They were responsible for the well-being of the people. A whole priesthood developed to conduct the elaborate worship necessary to keep the gods happy. Epic myths were read at ritual festivals to celebrate the triumph of good over evil.

Though they shared many ideas and even deities, Near Eastern mythologies were distinct. The agricultural Sumerians in their well-irrigated valleys focused on earth rather than sky gods. They believed people had been created as laborers for the gods. The Assyrians were a warlike people, and their gods and heroes were just as fierce. Babylonian myths explored immortality, while the Hittites had a tradition of disappearing gods. The Canaanites' belief that their powerful supreme god, El, lived in a remote mountain home was unusual for Mesopotamia. And the Persian prophet Zarathustra (c. 628–551 B.C.E.) introduced Zoroastrianism's dualism: that everything is part of the battle between good and evil. That struggle between the two is an important part of Near Eastern myth, which no doubt reflects its history of invasions and its geography of unpredictable river flows and harsh extremes.

Opposite: Palace at Persepolis, Iran

*▲ Some Persian creation myths say that Zurvan (center), the androgynous god of eternal time, gave birth to the twins **Ahura Mazda** and **Ahriman**. Zurvan proclaimed that the first of his sons to be born would rule. Ahriman pushed and tore his way out of the womb to win, but his reign of evil will only last 9,000 years before good triumphs.*

~

Ahura Mazda's son Atar fought a pitched battle against **Ahriman**'s creation, Azhi Dahaka. Dahaka was a monstrous, three-headed, six-eyed dragon. Lizards and scorpions crawled all over his body. Atar managed to chain up the beast in a mountain, but at the end of the world Dahaka will ravage one-third of the earth before he is finally destroyed.

ADAPA When the first man created by the Babylonian god **Ea** went out fishing, a squall capsized his boat. Adapa was furious and broke the south wind god's wing. The supreme sky god, Anu, was alarmed by a mortal this strong. He summoned Adapa to heaven. Ea warned him that it would be deadly to eat or drink anything there. Adapa charmed the gods, and Anu invited him to their feast. Adapa refused—and turned down immortality, which was the food and drink Anu offered.

AHRIMAN The god of light and wisdom, **Ahura Mazda,** wanted to make Persia a paradise on Earth. His evil twin was bent on destroying it. Ahriman dwelt in darkness and spewed out death, disease, and disorder. Whatever good his brother created, he undercut. When Ahura Mazda created life, Ahriman brought death. He countered truth with lies, summer with winter, fire with smoke, domestic animals with deadly ones. The twin gods symbolize the fight between good and evil. "Between them the right chose wisely, but not fools," said the Zoroastrian prophet Zarathustra.

AHURA MAZDA This Wise Lord and supreme god of Persia created a divine hierarchy, including the Seven Bounteous Immortals: Good Mind, Truth, Obedience, Devotion, Kingdom, Integrity, and Immortality, who sit beside him on gold thrones.

Then he made the universe, ending his work by creating the first human, **Gayomart.** Ahura Mazda's ideal world lasted several thousand years before it was attacked by his evil twin, **Ahriman.** After centuries of conflict, the god of light and truth will once again "reign and do everything according to his pleasure."

AN The great Sumerian gods came from this sky god and his mate, Ki, the earth goddess. He ruled as king of the gods in heaven, overseeing the divine court and appointing the mortal king of the Sumerians.

ANAT The Canaanite goddess of love and fertility did not shirk from her other role as warrior. She wielded a battle-ax and spear with zeal. When her brother-husband, **Baal,** died because of **Mot,** Anat went after this god of the underworld. She begged for Baal's return. Mot refused, so she slashed him with her sword, winnowed, scorched, and then ground his remains with a millstone, and scattered the pieces in a field where the birds ate them. Both Baal and Mot were eventually restored to life, and the cycle started all over. It symbolized winter changing to spring and celebrated the act of seeding and harvesting.

ASHUR When the Assyrians dominated Mesopotamia, so did their god of war. Ashur eclipsed the Babylonian **Marduk.** His cult was militaristic: Chained prisoners of war were often paraded through the streets of his city. He was usually shown inside a winged disk, poised with a bow and arrow.

ASTARTE This Phoenician goddess of love has several aspects— and different husbands with each. As Athirat, the lady of the sea, she is the wife of **El,** the mother of 70 gods (including **Baal**), and the queen of heaven. As Anat, the lady of the mountain, she is married to Baal. She was often worshiped as a sacred pole or pillar, considered a tree of life.

BAAL The Rider on the Clouds, the storm god of the Canaanites, took his mighty lightning-forked spear and charged into battle with the sea god Yam. He quickly dispatched Yam and his watery chaos, established order, and declared himself supreme. He even denied the powers of **Mot** and banished this lord of drought and death to the desert, forbidding him to cross any fertile lands. Mot was outraged and commanded Baal to appear in his kingdom—the underworld. Baal descended in terror and died the instant he was forced to eat mud, the food of the dead. His father, **El,** and all the gods went into mourning. Since Baal was also a fertility god, all rain and vegetation died off with him until **Anat** slew Mot, and Baal's corpse revived.

EA The Babylonian god of water, whom the Sumerians called **Enki,** is also a trickster god. He cheated **Adapa** out of immortality. And when the creator gods threatened to destroy the whole human race by flood, Ea warned **Utanapishtim.** In the same Sumerian myth, Enki is ordered not to contact people directly to tell them about the flood. So instead he whispers a warning into the reed wall of a palace, saving King Ziusudra and his family.

EL The dignified, bearded old king sits on his throne, crowned with bull horns, signs of his great strength. This is the usual depiction of the supreme god of the Canaanites who created all things before retiring to his remote home on Mount Saphon.

ENKI This Sumerian water god created the world, along with his wife **Ninhursaga,** the earth goddess, **An,** the god of heaven, and **Enlil,** the air god. When the gods complained about how tired they were of finding food, Enki made some clay servants—the first people. Enki rose up out of the seas, part man, part fish, and helped civilize these unruly human beings. He brought them tools, like the plow and the yoke, and taught them farming and crafts. He brought them letters and laws and taught them the ways of civilization. He directed the waters to provide irrigation and taught people how to build. The Babylonians called him **Ea.**

▶ *A bronze statue of **Astarte**, who is associated with **Ishtar.***

The mortal king Aqhat made a mortal mistake with the goddess Anat. She greatly coveted his magnificent bow and arrows and offered him gold, silver, and even immortality in exchange for the weapon. Aqhat scornfully replied, "Can women hunt with something like that?" Anat was furious and sent an eagle to kill Aqhat. The bow was lost in the fray.

Gilgamesh *was said to be one-third mortal, two-thirds divine. His exploits are told in the Sumerian epic* Gilgamesh. *The oldest story in the world, it was first written down around 2000 B.C.E., in cunieform that filled 12 clay tablets. This colossal stone relief guarded the throne of the King of Assur, c. 722–705 B.C.E.*

ENKIDU The people of Uruk were irritated with their hard-driving, powerful king **Gilgamesh,** so the gods sent this brawny, shaggy-haired champion to help rein him in. After a wrestling match, the wild man and the king acknowledged each other's great strength and became friends. They went off on many adventures until Enkidu was killed by the gods for his part in the slaying of the bull of heaven. Gilgamesh was grief-stricken and refused to bury Enkidu for so long that a worm fell out of the corpse's nose.

ENLIL This Sumerian-Babylonian god of air had ambiguous feelings about the people of Earth. He gave them the pickax so they could build and farm, but when they became too numerous in their noisy cities, he complained about the racket. Enlil tried to rid himself of all the disturbance by sending plague, drought, and finally a flood. Only one man, **Utanapishtim,** escaped his wrath.

ERESHKIGAL The divine queen of the Mesopotamian underworld was as dark as her sister **Inanna** was light. She ruled over the land of no return with her husband, **Nergal.** One myth says that when they fell in love, Ereshkigal threatened to release all the dead and let them overwhelm the living if Anu, the Babylonian sky god, did not allow Nergal to become her husband.

GAYOMART This primal man existed for 3,000 years before his meditating spirit was joined with a body. The Persian god **Ahura Mazda** created him; the wicked god **Ahriman** killed him. Forty years later, a plant grew from Gayomart's seed. It split and became the father and mother of the human race.

GILGAMESH Life as a king and adventurer was not enough for this great Mesopotamian hero. He wanted immortality, too. Gilgamesh and his friend **Enkidu** defeated the forest-dwelling, fire-breathing giant, Humbab. This caught the attention of the goddess **Ishtar,** who was smitten with the handsome king. When Gilgamesh rejected her advances, Ishtar had the gods send down the savage bull of heaven to ravage his kingdom. Enkidu seized its tail, and Gilgamesh slew it. Enkidu then bore the gods' wrath and died, too. Faced with this great loss and his own mortality, Gilgamesh traveled across the treacherous sea of death to find **Utanapishtim** and learn the secret of immortality. He told Gilgamesh to gather the plant called Never Grow Old from the bottom of the sea. The king did and headed home with the sweet-smelling leaves. But when Gilgamesh stopped to rest, a snake slithered up and swallowed the plant. The king dissolved into bitter tears when he saw the snake shed its skin. His chance at immortality was gone forever.

INANNA This powerful Sumerian goddess of love and fertility suddenly decided to pay her sister **Ereshkigal** a visit—in hopes of stealing her throne. As Inanna descended into the underworld, she passed through seven gates and was forced to strip off a piece of clothing or jewelry at each until she stood naked before her sister's throne. Ereshkigal turned her into a corpse and hung her up on a hook. Through **Enki's** wiles, Inanna was eventually restored to life, but she had to send her husband and another sister, alternately, to stand in her place. The same myth was later told about the Bablyonian goddess **Ishtar.**

ISHTAR She made love and war passionately. The Assyrian-Babylonian goddess of love could bring fertility to people and nations. As a goddess of war she sometimes grew a beard and was often pictured with a bow and quiver, charging into battle astride a lion. Just like her counterpart **Inanna,** she once boldly descended into the underworld.

MARDUK When **Tiamat,** the dreadful she-dragon of chaos, terrorized the Babylonian gods, only Marduk was willing to fight back— if the others made him the supreme deity. In a raging battle, Marduk ensnared Tiamat in his net. The ferocious dragon opened her jaws to swallow him, but the warrior blew a hurricane into her mouth so she couldn't close it. He shot an arrow into her mouth and killed her. Marduk carved up Tiamat's carcass to create the universe. He also slew her husband, Apsu, mixed clay with his blood, and created people.

MITHRA His name means *friend,* but this most popular of Persian deities is a virile war god. A champion of truth, law, and order, Mithra would let loose his deadly arrows and an even deadlier, bone-crunching boar against his enemies. Mithra is often shown slaying a bull, perhaps to ensure fertile prosperity. Bull sacrifice and complicated initiation rites were important parts of the Mithraic mystery religion that later developed throughout the Roman Empire.

▼ *The Gate of Ishtar, now housed in the state museum of Berlin, Germany, was built in Babylon during the reign of King Nebuchadnezzar II (605–562 B.C.E.). Its thousands of glazed brick tiles form elaborate borders and feature lions, bulls, dragons, and other mythical animals. It stood on the route of the great ancient New Year's processional honoring* **Marduk.**

Marduk declared Babylon the center of the universe. The Babylonians worshiped him as their national god and believed their fortunes were tied to his power. Each New Year they celebrated Marduk's exploits with an 11-day festival. The high priest had to recite the *Enuma elish* ("When on high"), the epic of creation that ran more than 1,000 lines. There was also a great procession of the gods. Statues of all the Mesopotamian gods were carried along a sacred route to the temple that housed a magnificent gold statue of Marduk.

❧

▶ *Mesopotamians and Persians believed that genies could help protect them from evil. Images of these guardian spirits were often found on temple walls and and at palace entrances. These magnificent stone genies from the Assyrian palace of Ashurnasirpal II in Nimrud were sculpted in the 9th century B.C.E. They are ten feet tall.*

MOT The Canaanite god of death and drought was locked in an eternal battle with the god of fertility, **Baal.** Their struggle and subsequent deaths and resurrections were ritualistic myths that celebrated seasonal and agricultural cycles.

NERGAL The Babylonian god of war didn't bother to rise when one of **Erishkigal**'s envoys came to a divine banquet. The angry goddess demanded that Nergal descend to her underworld. She threatened to kill him; he threatened to slit her throat. Erishkigal gave in after Nergal seized her by the hair and pulled her off her throne. He joined her in ruling the underworld.

NINHURSAGA The Sumerian earth goddess was annoyed at her husband **Enki**'s interest in their daughters. She grew eight special

plants, which Enki ate. He fell deathly ill with eight afflictions. Ninhursaga cursed her mate and fled. Enki paid a fox to find and return his wife to their Edenic paradise. Ninhursaga then cured him by giving birth to eight more gods.

RASHNU When a person died, his or her soul sat by the corpse for three days, awaiting judgment from this Persian god. He impartially weighed the soul's worth on golden scales. The good were led off to heaven by a beautiful woman; the bad were forced across a razor-thin bridge until they fell off into hell.

SHAMASH As he traveled across the sky in either a chariot or a solar barque, the Babylonian sun god saw everything. Therefore he was also the god of justice. He helped restore **Baal** to life and was worshiped by the Sumerians as Utu.

SIN The Sumerian moon god and son of **Enlil** ruled the calendar. Waning and waxing of the moon was a continual cycle of underworld demons chasing the moon and worshipers sacrificing for his restoration.

TAMMUZ The Babylonian god of spring and vegetation was married to the goddess **Ishtar.** Every year he descended to the underworld in her place. The earth withered until he rose again in the spring.

TELIPINU Some myths say he got lost in a desert; some say he ran off so angrily he put his boots on the wrong feet. But all myths agree that when this Hittite god of agriculture disappeared, no plant grew, no animal gave birth. Nature just dried up, starved, or died. His mother sent a bee to find Telipinu. The insect stung him out of a stupor, and he flew home on an eagle to restore the earth.

TESHUB One of the most important Hittite deities was this warrior god of weather and storms who wielded a thunder ax and lightning bolts. Teshub dethroned his father, who then sired a stone giant to avenge him. The giant stood 9,000 leagues tall and 9,000 leagues wide.

TIAMAT In the beginning there was only this goddess of salt water, and Apsu, the god of fresh water. When the waters mingled, they created the first four Babylonian gods. The divine offspring were noisy. Apsu planned to destroy them but was instead slain by their son **Ea.** Tiamat, as a horrific she-dragon, then gave birth to all sorts of monsters like toothed serpents, centaurs, and lion-headed demons. They attacked the terrified gods, who convinced **Marduk** to fight their battle. The mighty warrior killed Tiamat and split her "like a shellfish" to create heaven and Earth.

UTANAPISHTIM Rains lashed the earth for seven days and nights. The floodwaters rose and drowned all living things except this Babylonian and his ark. He had survived because the kind god **Ea** warned him of the angry god **Enlil's** coming deluge. Utanapishtim built a cube-shaped ark and filled it with his family, wild animals, gold, and silver. After a week of deluge, he sent out a dove and a swallow. Both birds returned to the ark. Then he sent out a raven, which did not. He then knew the floodwaters were subsiding and the bird had landed. Utanapishtim disembarked, offered sacrifice to the gods, and was rewarded with immortality. This Babylonian flood story is similiar to the Sumerian story of King Ziusudra and predates the biblical story of Noah by nearly 1,000 years.

▲ *Worshipers bring offerings to the sun god* **Shamash** *in this 9th-century* B.C.E. *relief. His symbol, a solar disk with a four-pointed star, sits on an altar in front of him. The lettering in the background is cuneiform.*

Deciphering Near Eastern myths and their meanings is a complicated and controversial job. Most of the myths were written on clay tablets. Many have been lost, and the ones discovered are often just fragments. There are also problems translating dead languages. Cuneiform, the wedge-shaped symbol writing of the Sumerians and the Akkadians, was not decoded until the 19th century.

GREECE

Always to be best and to be distinguished above the rest.

—Homer, *The Iliad*

No one had a greater impact on the Western world than the Greeks. From the Parthenon to a Picasso painting, their myths and legends influenced every form of Western art, architecture, and literature. The Greeks even gave us the very word *myth*, from *mythos*, meaning imaginative story.

Mythic life was part of real life for the ancient Greeks. They built beautiful temples to honor their gods and goddesses. They visited sacred sanctuaries for the gods' advice on personal or political matters. They created complex family trees that linked kings, heroes, and immortals, and could be used to explain Greece's rich history.

Mortals and Immortals

The peoples of many ancient civilizations bowed down to a remote or almighty god-king, whose rule they never questioned. The Greeks put human beings in this powerful position. The Athenians even invented democracy, a radical idea in 5th century B.C.E.

Greek mythology reflects this humanism. Many Greek myths are about extraordinary but mortal heroes and heroines from a past era. In their divine myths, the Greeks made their gods and goddesses immortal, endowed them with remarkable powers—and gave them very human personalities! Gods and goddesses are wise, rash, heroic, unfaithful, jealous, fair, and vengeful. They feast, make love, and fight wars with zest.

The Poets and the Pantheon

For centuries, Greek myths were memorized, sung or recited. In the 8th century B.C.E., Homer (c. 700–750 B.C.E.) composed the epic poems the *Iliad* and the *Odyssey*, and Hesiod (700s B.C.E.), the *Theogeny*. Both helped establish the classical Olympian pantheon.

The Olympians Triumph

Greek mythology has several creation myths. In the Olympian myth cycle, Gaia, the Earth, and Uranus, the sky, spawned the one-eyed Cyclopes, the 100-handed Giants, and the enormous Titans. Cronus, the youngest Titan, overthrew his father, and married his sister Rhea. He swallowed their first five children to make sure history didn't repeat itself. Rhea secretly gave birth to one more child, Zeus. He dethroned Cronus, forcing him to vomit up Hestia, Demeter, Hera, Hades, and Poseidon. They joined their brother Zeus, the 100-handed Giants, and the Cyclopes in a mighty battle against the Titans. The war raged for ten years. The Olympians triumphed and then divided up the universe. They were called the Olympians because most of them lived in magnificent palaces atop Mount Olympus, the highest mountain in Greece. Aphrodite and a second generation of Olympians, Apollo, Artemis, Ares, Hermes, Athena, Hephaestus, (and later Dionysus), completed the pantheon.

The immortal world also included lesser gods and semi-divine beings, usually the children of a mortal woman and a god. The fortunes of mortals and immortals were tightly woven together. And everyone's future—man, woman, god, goddess—was ruled by the Fates.

Opposite: The Parthenon on the Acropolis, Athens, Greece

▲ *Greek warriors in the Trojan Horse; clay vase, 7th century* B.C.E.

❧

The Trojan War was not only fought by mortals; most of the Olympians were also embroiled. Gods and goddesses stirred up trouble, switched allegiances, and tricked mortals and each other. **Hera, Athena,** and **Poseidon** backed the Greeks; **Ares, Aphrodite, Apollo,** and **Artemis** backed the Trojans. **Zeus** tried to be neutral but favored the Trojans, who also had the Amazons, the legendary women warriors, on their side. The Greeks were so violent when they jumped out of the Trojan Horse that **Athena** and **Poseidon** turned against them.

ACHILLES A moody ally and a vengeful enemy, this fearless Greek warrior is the central figure in Homer's epic poem the *Iliad*. He withdrew from the Trojan War after being insulted by the Greek commander **Agamemnon** but returned to battle **Hector** in single combat. He killed the Trojan prince, tied the corpse to his chariot, and dragged it three times around the walls of Troy. Achilles was later shot through the heel by **Paris,** Hector's brother.

ADONIS When **Aphrodite** first saw the beautiful baby Adonis, she fell madly in love. She put him in a chest and gave him to **Persephone** for safekeeping. The queen of the underworld also fell under Adonis's spell and refused to give him back to the goddess of love. Zeus settled the matter. The handsome youth

was to divide his time between the two goddesses. One day while hunting, Adonis was killed by a wild boar (which may have been a jealous **Ares** in disguise). Anemone flowers sprang up where his blood dripped.

AGAMEMNON The king of Mycenae tricked his wife, **Clytemnestra,** into sending him their daughter, Iphigenia. He sacrificed the young girl to **Artemis** so that the goddess would calm the north wind and let the Greek fleet sail off to the Trojan War. Agamemnon was chosen to lead the Greek army but then alienated the Greeks' best fighter, **Achilles,** by taking his mistress. He survived the ten-year war, returned home to a royal welcome, and was then murdered by his angry wife.

AJAX This mighty Greek warrior battled the Trojan **Hector** for an entire day before they both respectfully withdrew swords in honor of each other's prowess. Ajax was later furious at not being awarded the slain **Achilles'** splendid armor. That night he went mad, slaughtering cows and sheep he thought were his fellow Greeks. In the morning, when he realized what he had done, he killed himself out of shame.

ANDROMEDA This hapless young girl was to be sacrificed because her mother had angered **Poseidon** with her boasting. Andromeda was chained to a rock, waiting to be devoured by a serpent, when **Perseus** flew over. He slew the monster and married the maiden.

ANTAEUS As long as this Giant touched the earth (his mother, **Gaia**), no one could beat him at wrestling. He challenged all strangers to a match and then added the losers' skulls to his temple. The Giant was finally defeated by **Heracles,** who wrenched him from the earth and lifted him sky-high.

ANTIGONE She wandered the earth with her blind, banished father, **Oedipus.** After his death, the sad maiden returned home to Thebes only to find the rest of her family at war with each other. When Antigone defied royal orders not to bury her slain brother, her own uncle had her buried alive.

APHRODITE Born of the sea's foam and **Uranus's** blood, this Olympian was the goddess of love and beauty. She used her magic girdle to control and complicate everyone's love life, even that of **Zeus.** She constantly sent him chasing after women and **nymphs,** thereby making an archenemy of Zeus's jealous wife, **Hera.** Beautiful as she was, Aphrodite was married to the lame, ugly blacksmith god, **Hephaestus.** This did not stop her numerous affairs, and she bore children by **Ares, Hermes,** and **Poseidon.**

APOLLO To the Greeks, this youthful, beautiful Olympian god of the sun, music, poetry, medicine, philosophy, science, and archery represented the spirit of their culture. In fact, they called him by more than 300 different titles of honor!

Apollo was the son of **Zeus** and the Titaness Leto, and was the twin of **Artemis.** As a child, he slew the fearful serpent Python at Delphi and took over the oracle there. He traveled in a chariot drawn by swans and was famous for his beautiful lyre-playing.

ARACHNE Bragging always brings down the wrath of the gods, so when this mortal maiden boasted of her weaving skills, **Athena** naturally challenged her to a contest. Arachne then wove a beautiful tapestry that was bound to displease all the gods: It showed their love affairs! Athena knocked her on the head with a shuttle and turned the foolish girl into a spider.

The Trojan War started with an apple. The goddess of discord tossed a golden fruit into an Olympian banquet. It was addressed to the most beautiful goddess. Hera, Athena, and Aphrodite all quickly claimed it. Zeus decided that a Trojan prince, Paris, should award the apple. All three goddesses bribed him. Hera would make Paris ruler of Asia; Athena would make him victorious in all battles; and Aphrodite promised him marriage to Helen, the world's most beautiful woman. Paris gave Aphrodite the golden apple and went to Greece after Helen. Unfortunately she was already married. Their elopement sparked the Trojan War. (And Aphrodite's rivals, Hera and Athena, were more than happy to help trounce the Trojans!)

◄ Apollo and Daphne, *a bronze sculpture by Gianlorenzo Bernini (1598–1680, Italian), shows the nymph escaping the god's embrace. Her father, a river god, turned Daphne into a laurel tree. The brokenhearted* **Apollo** *made its leaves sacred. The Greeks used laurel wreaths to crown poets and athletes.*

A family tree of *all* the Greek gods and goddesses would have more branches (and roots!) than could fit here. The Greek pantheon was headed by the Olympians (including Dionysus, who replaced Hestia as an Olympian in the 5th century B.C.E.). The 12 Olympians are:

- Zeus
- Hera
- Athena
- Apollo
- Artemis
- Aphrodite
- Ares
- Demeter
- Hephaestus
- Hestia/Dionysus
- Hermes
- Poseidon

Hades was an important god, but he lived in the underworld, not on Mount Olympus, so he is usually not counted among the 12.

▶ *When **Athena**'s father, **Zeus** (center), complained of a headache, his forehead was split with an ax and out sprang the warrior goddess—in helmet and full armor! Grecian vase, 6th century B.C.E.*

ARES Everyone hated him: gods, mortals, poets, even his own mother, **Hera.** This god of war enjoyed bloody, violent battles. His traveling companions included his sister, Discord, and his nephew, Strife. **Aphrodite** alone loved Ares. The couple had two children before **Zeus** forbade their affair.

ARGONAUTS These 50 adventurers set sail aboard the *Argo* with **Jason** at the helm and **Heracles, Castor and Polydeuces, Orpheus,** and **Theseus** among the crew. They were headed to Colchis, on the Black Sea, to capture the Golden Fleece. One of the *Argo*'s oak timbers came from **Zeus**'s sacred grove. It could talk and helped guide the sailors on their perilous voyage.

ARTEMIS The Lady of the Wild Things was **Apollo**'s twin. She asked her father, **Zeus,** to let her remain a virgin—and to give her all the mountains in the world. She ordered the **Cyclopes** to make her a silver bow and arrow. Then she spent most of her time roaming the woods as goddess of the hunt.

ATHENA She is the goddess of wisdom, the crafts, and the protector of cities, especially her namesake, Athens. Athena and **Poseidon** both claimed Athens as their city. The gods decided the winner would be whoever created the most useful thing for the Athenians. Poseidon struck a rock and a saltwater spring flowed. Athena grew an olive tree. She won. The Athenians built the famous Parthenon (447–438 B.C.E.) in honor of their patroness. Inside the temple was a 40-foot-high gold-and-ivory statue of the goddess.

ATLAS This **Titan** was punished for siding against the Olympians in the war between gods and Titans. He was condemned to hold up the enormous weight of the sky for eternity.

BELLEROPHON Heroes can be fearless and foolish! This noble prince mounted his winged steed, **Pegasus,** and slew the Chimera, a fantastic fire-breathing beast with the head of a lion, the body of a goat, and the tail of a serpent. He later grew too ambitious and tried to ride Pegasus up Mount Olympus so he could join the gods. **Zeus** was outraged. He sent a fly to sting Pegasus, who bucked and hurtled Bellerophon down to Earth.

CASTOR AND POLYDEUCES
Sons of **Leda,** these devoted brothers were inseparable. Castor (whose father was mortal) was killed in a quarrel. Polydeuces was inconsolable and did not want to outlive his brother, but he was immortal because his father was **Zeus.** Zeus decided to let the brothers stay together, one day in heaven, the next on Earth. He also honored them with two stars, the Gemini (twins).

CHARON He is a gloomy old boatman who rows the dead across the river Styx into **Hades.** The dead had to be buried properly, with coins on their eyes or under their tongues. Otherwise Charon would refuse to take them, and their pale ghosts would wander the Styxian shores.

CHIRON Centaurs are half man, half horse, and Chiron is the noblest of these usually unruly creatures. He was the wise teacher of **Jason,** Actaeon, **Achilles,** and Asclepius. **Heracles** accidently wounded the centaur. Rather than live in pain for eternity, Chiron died, sacrificing his immortality for **Prometheus**'s release.

CIRCE She had her own island, her own palace, and her own peculiar custom of wining and dining visitors and then turning them into pigs. **Odysseus** outwitted the enchantress with a magic herb from **Hermes.** Circe released his

men but charmed Odysseus into spending a year with her.

CLYTEMNESTRA The wife of King **Agamemnon** is one of Greek drama's great tragic figures. After Agamemnon sacrificed their daughter, Iphigenia, Clytemnestra mourned—and vowed revenge! Her husband returned after the ten-year Trojan War, and she greeted him as a royal hero. Then she prepared his bath and wrapped him in a net shirt with no sleeves. Agamemnon was trapped. Her lover, Aegisthus, stabbed him, and in some accounts, Clytemnestra then chopped off her husband's head. Her son, **Orestes,** later completed the violent family cycle by killing his mother.

▲ Jason and His Teacher *by Maxfield Parrish (1870–1966, American). The centaur* **Chiron** *taught Jason and all his pupils hunting, medicine, and other useful skills.*

☙

Atlas left his mark on geography. There is a mountain range in northwest Africa called the Atlas Mountains; and in the 16th century, Gerhardus Mercator (1512–1594, Flemish), a famous mathematician and mapmaker, first used the word *atlas* to mean a collection of maps.

Like **Demeter,** the other great earth deity, **Dionysus** is associated with a seasonal cycle of death and rebirth. He was honored with a great festival held every spring in Athens. It included a three-day drama contest during which playwrights such as Aeschylus (525–456 B.C.E.), Sophocles (496–406 B.C.E.), and Euripides (484–406 B.C.E.) staged some of the world's greatest tragedies at the theater of Dionysus on the Acropolis.

～

▼ *Dionysus was said to have invented wine, so he's often shown with a grapevine. This detail from a clay kylix, or drinking vessel (6th century B.C.E.), may also refer to a story about pirates kidnapping the god. He turned their mast into a vine, their oars into snakes, and the pirates themselves into dolphins.*

CRONUS The youngest **Titan,** he overthrew his father, **Uranus,** married his sister, Rhea, then ate all their children so none of them could overthrow *him.* Rhea bore her youngest child secretly in Crete, then wrapped up a stone and fed this to her husband instead. Her clever actions saved the life of **Zeus,** who dethroned Cronus and forced him to throw up all Zeus's siblings. Cronus later ruled the Elysian Fields in **Hades.**

CYCLOPES Though they each only had one eye, these Giants were skilled craftsworkers. They forged **Zeus**'s mighty thunderbolt, **Hades'** magic helmet of invisibility, and **Poseidon**'s trident. Zeus protected these huge creatures, since the Cyclopes had helped fight the Olympian gods' war against the **Titans.**

DAEDALUS This renowned Athenian architect became a prisoner in his own greatest building: the labyrinth. Daedalus designed this elaborate maze for King **Minos** of Crete, who hid the Minotaur in it. He later revealed the labyrinth's secret, which let **Theseus** kill the monster and escape the maze. Minos then imprisoned Daedalus and his son, **Icarus,** in the labyrinth. Only the father survived their escape attempt. Minos tracked him to a royal court in Sicily. He lured the clever inventor out of hiding with a puzzle: How can you get a thread through a snail's shell? Daedalus couldn't resist. He tied a thread to an ant and sent it walking through the shell. Then he outwitted his would-be captor by building a new set of pipes and drowning Minos in hot oil while he bathed.

DEMETER When her beloved only daughter, **Persephone,** was kidnapped, this goddess of agriculture left Olympus and wandered the earth for nine days and nights, searching for her. Finally, **Helios,** the sun god, told her the truth: Persephone had been seized by **Hades** and taken to the underworld. The grief-stricken goddess made the earth's crops wither. Animals died. The whole human race was threatened. **Zeus** negotiated a compromise, and Persephone and Demeter were reunited at Eleusis. This became a site of secret, sacred ceremonies, whose exact rituals remain a mystery to this day.

DIONYSUS Being a son of **Zeus** made this god's birth that much more difficult. **Hera** was jealous of his mother, Semele, so she told the girl to ask to see her lover Zeus in all his glory. The vision killed her, but not before Zeus grabbed the baby Dionysus and sewed him into his own thigh. When he was born, Hera ordered the **Titans** to chop him up and boil him, but Rhea restored him. He was then raised by **nymphs.** The last to become an Olympian, this god of vegetation and the vine commanded a strange cult. Centaurs, satyrs (half-man, half-goat beasts), nymphs, and maenads followed Dionysus in his travels through Greece, Egypt, India, and back. Their rites were wild, delirious, and often drunken. Kings like the Theban Pentheus found this behavior threatening. He forbid Dionysian celebrations—and forfeited his life. The angry god sent the king's own mother into a frenzied fit. She mistook her son for a wild animal and killed him.

ELECTRA She was like an orphan in her own home. Her mother, **Clytemnestra,** killed her father, **Agamemnon.** Electra spirited away her brother, **Orestes,** so he would not be killed, too. For seven long years she was neglected by her mother and humiliated by Clytemnestra's lover, Aegisthus. He made the girl marry a poor peasant and prevented her from having any children who might challenge him.

Electra and Orestes were reunited at their father's tomb and together avenged his death.

EROS The god of passionate love, mischievous Eros is usually depicted as a child with wings and a bow and arrow. However, in the famous love story about **Psyche,** Eros is a handsome youth. He is commonly considered the son of **Aphrodite** and **Ares.**

EUROPA The great god **Zeus** was struck by her beauty, and she was equally struck by his—since he appeared to her as a gentle, snow-white bull. The maiden threw flower wreaths on the animal's horns and climbed on its back. Then the bull immediately plunged into the sea with the terrified girl. Zeus swam to Crete and there became Europa's lover. She gave birth to three children, including **Minos.**

▲ The Abduction of Europa *by Pierre Bonnard (1867–1947, French) is one of many art masterpieces inspired by the myth.*

The Maenads dressed in animals skins, twined ivy wreaths in their hair, and danced themselves into a frenzy in honor of Dionysus. People feared these madwomen who roamed the mountains and could tear apart animals with their bare hands.

The Greek underworld had an interesting but shadowy geography. It was either deep in the earth or at the edge of the world. A three-headed, three-tailed dog, Cerberus, guarded the entrance, so that no dead souls could leave. Its rivers included the Styx, by which the gods swore their oaths; the Lethe, whose waters caused forgetfulness; and the Phlegeton, a river of fire. The dead were judged: Good souls went to the pleasurable Elysian Fields; indifferent souls went to the ghostly Asphodel Meadows; and the guilty suffered punishments in the depths of Tartarus.

FATES These three white-robed goddesses, also called the *Moirai*, determined the length and course of every human life. Clotho spun out each thread of destiny; Lachesis measured it to the right length; and Atropos snipped it with her shears.

FURIES The earth goddess **Gaia** was weary of **Uranus,** the overbearing sky god. She asked her son **Cronus** to separate the two of them with a sickle. Uranus bled onto the earth, and the Furies were born from the three drops. They were fierce creatures with whips who relentlessly hounded guilty mortals until they went mad. The ancients were afraid to even say their Greek name, *Erinyes*.

GAIA The ancient Mother Earth gave birth to **Uranus** and then became the sky god's passionate lover. Their offspring include the **Titans,** the **Cyclopes,** and the 100-handed Giants.

GANYMEDE This most beautiful of mortals was seduced by **Zeus,** disguised as an eagle. The bird then flew up to Olympus with the young Trojan prince, where he became cupbearer at the divine feasts.

HADES Unlike his fellow Olympians, the god of the dead ruled not from the heavens but from the underworld, which also bears his name. He rarely left his ghostly palace, but when he did, he usually donned the magic helmet of invisibility that the **Cyclopes** had made for him. Part of the year he shared his throne with **Persephone,** whom he kidnapped from **Demeter.**

HARPIES They had vultures' bodies, women's faces, and they were always hungry! These hideous creatures swooped down on their victims at meals and stole all the food with their sharp claws. What they couldn't snatch they befouled with their awful stench.

HECTOR The son of Troy's King **Priam,** he was a glorious hero of the Trojan War. He slew Patroclus, who was outfitted in his best friend **Achilles'** famous armor. This drew

◄ *Cerberus sits at the feet of* **Hades** *and* **Persephone,** *king and queen of the underworld, in this 15th-century French illuminated manuscript.*

the sulky Greek hero back into the war, and the Trojans were routed. Hector alone stood his ground. Achilles closed in, with **Athena** by his side. Hector then ran until Athena tricked him into imagining his brother was there to help him. He stopped and faced his enemy. By the time Hector realized the goddess's deceit, he was doomed.

HELEN Hers was the "face that launched a thousand ships" when her abduction sparked the Trojan War. She was the daughter of **Zeus** and **Leda** and was considered the most beautiful mortal woman in the world. Many a prince wanted to marry her. To prevent any jealous outbreaks, her father made each suitor vow to defend whomever Helen married. She chose to wed the Greek king Menelaus, brother of **Agamemnon.**

HELIOS A rooster crows each morning, and this sun god leaves his radiant palace in the east and drives his chariot west across the sky, bringing light to the world. Each night he sails home, asleep in a golden boat (or, some say, goblet) made by **Hephaestus.**

HEPHAESTUS He was ornery and ugly and the only Olympian god who got thrown out of heaven . . . twice! His mother, **Hera,** tossed him down from Olympus because he was such a repulsive-looking baby. Later he quarreled with **Zeus,** and he hurled him out, too. Hephaestus fell for one whole day before he landed. The blow made him lame.

Dessins lithographiques
Paul Gauguin

Nevertheless, this god of fire and the forge was an incredibly talented metalworker. He built golden mechanical women who could think and talk. His three-legged stools could run on their own. In his hot, sooty, volcanic smithy, Hephaestus forged Zeus's famous aegis and **Achilles'** fateful armor, and made palaces, weapons, and ornaments for the gods.

HERA She was queen of heaven, daughter of the **Titans, Cronus** and Rhea, and married to her brother, **Zeus.** In her often unjust, jealous rages, she would go to great lengths to punish the lovers and children of her adulterous husband. She and Zeus quarreled and bickered constantly, despite which Hera is the goddess of wives and marriage.

▲ *This lithograph by Paul Gauguin (1848–1903, French) was based on the myth of* **Leda***, mother of* **Castor and Polydeuces, Helen,** *and* **Clytemnestra.**

Achilles' own death had been foretold long before he slew **Hector.** His mother, Thetis, dipped her baby in the River Styx so he would become invulnerable, but forgot that her hand covered Achilles' heel (a phrase that now means a weak spot). In battle, even Achilles' talking horse warned him of his impending death.

The 12 Labors of **Heracles** are:

⟡ The **Nemean Lion** was invulnerable to wounds. Heracles wrestled it to death. He wore its skin as his armor ever after.

⟡ The **Hydra** had nine heads and breath that could kill. Heracles chopped off the heads and had his nephew brand the wounds, so new heads wouldn't grow.

⟡ The **Cerynean Hind.** It took Heracles a year to capture this gold-horned animal, which couldn't be killed because it was sacred to Artemis.

⟡ The **Erymanthian Boar.** Heracles tracked the beast, tired it out in the snow, then carried it back on his shoulder alive. King Eurystheus jumped in a jar when he saw the hero coming.

⟡ The **Stymphalian Birds** were vultures that destroyed everything in their path. Heracles flushed them out with castanets made by **Hephaestus,** then shot them with poison arrows.

⟡ The **Augean Stables** housed hundreds of cattle and had not been cleaned in years. Heracles had one day to clean the yards. He did it by diverting two rivers.

(continues on next page)

HERACLES Stories about Greece's greatest hero have inspired ancient poets and modern moviemakers. His size and strength are legendary: As a baby he strangled two serpents in his crib; as an adult, he stood eight feet tall. Heracles was **Zeus**'s son, which automatically made him **Hera**'s foe. She drove him into an insane fit, during which he killed his wife and children. After consulting the oracle at Delphi, the hero promised to serve King Eurystheus of Tiryns for 12 years to atone for his heinous crime. He then performed his famous 12 Labors. Some years later, Heracles' second wife unwittingly sent him a poison shirt, to keep him from deserting her. The hero could not remove the deadly shirt and in agony climbed up on his own funeral pyre. He was then taken to Olympus where he joined the immortals.

HERMES With his winged cap and sandals, this Olympian is the swiftest of the gods. He seemed to be everywhere and is included in more myths than any other god. As a baby he stole **Apollo**'s oxen and then invented the lyre from a tortoiseshell as a gift of penance. One of his grimmer jobs was to bring the dead to **Hades.**

HESTIA As goddess of the hearth, this Olympian was honored in all Greek homes. She was a virgin goddess who, unlike her fellow deities, did not interfere in the affairs of people. She was later replaced by **Dionysus** in the Olympic pantheon.

ICARUS This youth and his father, **Daedalus,** were imprisoned in the labyrinth by King Minos. Daedalus made two pairs of wings from feathers and beeswax. His instructions were simple: Fly out of the labyrinth, but don't fly too close to the sun. Icarus ignored him and soared into the sky. The sun melted the beeswax, the wings broke, and the boy plunged to his death.

JASON Although he was a prince, he had been cheated out of his inheritance. Jason came to reclaim the throne at Iolcus, but his uncle Pelias ordered him to bring back the Golden Fleece of Colchis first. After a harrowing sea journey with the **Argonauts,** he reached Colchis, where the king ordered yet another ordeal. Jason had to harness fire-breathing bulls to plow a field, then sow it with serpent's teeth that would immediately grow into bloodthirsty soldiers. Luckily **Medea,** the Colchian princess, fell madly in love with the hero and shared her magic with him. Jason subdued the bulls, sowed the deadly seeds, and then threw a stone at the soldiers so they all fought with one another. But he still had to get the fleece—which was guarded by a fierce, thousand-coiled dragon. Medea lulled the dragon to sleep with a song, and Jason snatched the Golden Fleece.

LEDA This beautiful queen of Sparta was seduced by **Zeus** who had changed himself into a swan. In some accounts, Leda laid two eggs: one held **Polydeuces** and **Helen,** the other **Castor** and **Clytemnestra.** Other versions say that Castor and Clytemnestra are Leda's mortal children by her husband, the king.

MEDEA She was equally passionate as lover or enemy. This Colchian princess betrayed her father and killed her brother to help **Jason** win the Golden Fleece. When Jason later abandoned her and their two sons, she murdered his new bride with a flesh-eating robe, then killed the children.

MEDUSA One look at her hideous face would turn anyone into stone. The only mortal Gorgon, she had deadly poisonous blood running in her left side and blood that could restore life flowing in her right side. She was beheaded by the hero **Perseus,** who presented the head to the Gorgon's enemy, **Athena.** The goddess put it on her shield.

🕉 The *Cretan Bull* belched fire, but Heracles still caught it single-handed.

🕉 The *Diomedes' Horses* were flesh-eaters, so Heracles fed them their master and then easily harnessed them.

🕉 *Hippolyte's Girdle* belonged to the queen of the Amazons. She willingly gave it to Heracles, but **Hera** stirred up trouble. A battle ensued, and Heracles killed Hippolyte.

🕉 The *Cattle of Geryon.* To get them, the hero had to first kill their three headed, three-bodied, six-handed owner. En route back he created the Rock of Gibraltar.

🕉 *Cerberus.* Heracles had to capture the fierce three-headed guard dog of Hades with his bare hands. Then he had to return the beast—the king was terrified by it!

🕉 The *Apples of Hesperides.* Harvesting this fruit meant killing the 100-headed dragon that guarded the apple tree.

◄ *Heracles battles the nine-headed Hydra.*

▶ *Caravaggio's (1573–1610, Italian) Head of Medusa captures the Gorgon monster's frightful glare. The Gorgons were a hideous trio. With their boar tusks, huge claws, and snake hair, these three sisters were terrifying enough to turn people into stone with a single glance.*

〜

Asclepius, the son of **Apollo** was born after his mother died and later became famous for raising the dead himself. A learned doctor, Asclepius used **Medusa**'s blood, which he got from **Athena**, to help him restore life. **Hades** and **Zeus** became furious: Asclepius was keeping souls from the underworld. Zeus struck him dead with a thunderbolt.

〜

Never to speak, only to repeat, that was Echo's sad fate. Her chattering distracted **Hera** when the goddess was trying to catch **Zeus** in a tryst. The goddess punished the nymph. She could never again talk first but only echo what others said. The nymph later faded away to nothing but a voice after **Narcissus** rejected her love.

MIDAS The king of Phyrgia rescued Silenius, the close companion of **Dionysus.** The god offered the king a reward. Greedy Midas asked that everything he touch turn to gold. And it did—including his food, his drink, and his daughter! The remorseful (and hungry) king begged to have the spell lifted. Another time Midas unwisely chose **Pan** over **Apollo** in a musical contest, after which he suddenly sprouted huge donkey ears. Midas hid them under a cap and threatened his barber with death if he said anything. The barber was bursting with the news, so he dug a hole and whispered Midas's secret into it. Reeds grew up near the hole and repeated the secret until everyone knew the king's shame.

MINOS He should have sacrificed the bull sent by **Poseidon.** Instead, this king of Crete kept it, and the angry god made the Cretan queen, Pasiphae, lust after the animal. She then gave birth to the Minotaur, a half-man, half-bull monster. Minos imprisoned it in a labyrinth built by **Daedalus.** The powerful king forced the Athenians to send him young men and women, which he then fed to the Minotaur.

MUSES These nine beautiful, inspirational goddesses are the patrons of the arts. They were the daughters of **Zeus** and the **Titan** Mnemosyne, or Memory.

NARCISSUS This vain prince rejected all suitors, including the **nymph** Echo. He was punished by the gods, who made him fall in love with his own reflection. Every time he tried to embrace the watery image it disappeared.

NYMPHS Although these beautiful maidens are divine, they are not immortal. There are different kinds of nymphs, all connected to nature. Tree nymphs are called dryads and hamadryads; the naiads live in springs, lakes, and rivers; the oreads roam the mountains; the nereids swim in the sea.

ODYSSEUS The great Greek warrior king who is the main subject of Homer's epic poem the *Odyssey* spent ten years fighting the Trojan War and another ten trying to get home to his faithful wife, **Penelope,** and their son, Telemachus. He was famous for his clever, crafty ideas and was the one who talked the Greeks into building the infamous Trojan Horse. When he finally did reach his home in Ithaca, the warrior disguised himself as a beggar. The palace was overrun by loutish suitors. Odysseus outwitted them all in an archery contest and, with his son's help, killed them and regained control of his court.

OEDIPUS This unlucky Theban prince was abandoned at birth because an oracle said he would kill his father, King Laius, and marry his mother, Queen Jocasta. He was adopted by the king of Corinth but left his court as an adult. As he wandered, Oedipus unknowingly killed his real father in a roadside quarrel. Then he solved the riddle of the Sphinx, a frightful monster who devoured travelers outside the gates of Thebes. The Thebans offered him their throne and their now-widowed queen as thanks. Oedipus married Jocasta, his mother. When he found out that the horrible prophecy had been fulfilled, he blinded himself with her brooch.

ORESTES He was the son of the ill-fated **Agamemnon** and the ill-used **Clytemnestra.** His bitter sister, **Electra,** urged him to avenge their mother's murder of their father. But this sacred duty was a profane act in itself. Orestes consulted the oracle at Delphi, who confirmed his mission. He fulfilled his tragic destiny by stabbing his mother to death, for which he was relentlessly haunted by the **Furies.** Eventually, the goddess **Athena** appointed a court to decide his fate. With her favorable vote, she freed Orestes from the Furies.

ORION A son of **Poseidon,** this handsome youth was a mighty hunter who had seduced both a princess and Eos, goddess of the dawn. When he became a hunting companion of **Artemis,** her brother **Apollo** feared for his sister's chastity. He had a scorpion chase Orion out to sea. Back on shore, Apollo tricked Artemis into shooting a deadly arrow into the hunter, whom she mistook for an enemy.

One of the Cyclopes, Polyphemus, trapped **Odysseus** in his cave. Quick-witted Odysseus had his men sharpen a wooden stake in the fire. He got Polyphemus drunk and poked out his one eye. Then he and his men tied themselves to sheep. When blind Polyphemus let the flock out in the morning, he felt only fleece. Odysseus and his crew escaped.

❧

◄ Oedipus and the Sphinx *by Gustave Moreau (1826–1898, French). The Sphinx asked people this riddle: What animal goes on four feet in the morning, on two at noon, and on three in the evening? If they couldn't answer, she ate them. When she preyed upon* **Oedipus,** *he provided the riddle's answer: Man, because he crawls as a baby, walks as an adult, and uses a cane in old age. The Sphinx was humiliated at her loss and jumped off a cliff.*

▶ Pan feverishly chased the nymph Syrinx to a riverbank. She turned herself into a reed to escape the randy god. Pan couldn't tell which reed was his nymph, so he cut off several stalks, bound them together, and created the panpipe. He is often pictured playing the musical instrument, as in this painting, Faune Jouant de la Diaule by Pablo Picasso (1881–1973, Spanish).

❧

Some Greek myths say **Prometheus** molded the first mortals out of clay. Others talk about five ages or races of humans. The first, a golden race created by the **Titans,** lived in a peaceful, plentiful, Edenlike world; when they died, they became happy spirits. The Olympians created the second, silver race, but **Zeus** destroyed them all because they didn't sacrifice to the gods. The bronze race followed. They were such fierce warriors that they slaughtered themselves. The fourth, unnamed race were the mortal heroes of famous events such as the Trojan War; their souls passed on to the Elysian Fields. Ever since then, all people have belonged to an iron age. This age, filled with evil, sorrow, and a little bit of good, will also eventually die out.

ORPHEUS No one could play music more sweetly—he could make wild animals stop to listen, he could even overpower the **Sirens.** When his beloved wife, Eurydice, died, Orpheus went down to the underworld. His music charmed **Hades** himself into letting Eurydice leave, if Orpheus could lead his wife up to the earth without turning back to look at her. As the couple emerged from the darkness, Orpheus couldn't stand it anymore. He turned . . . and Eurydice vanished forever! Inconsolable, Orpheus wandered the world until he was killed by maenads.

PAN He had goat horns and legs, a tail, and a beard . . . at birth! This merry son of **Hermes** is a faun who loves **nymphs,** nature, and noise.

During the war against the **Titans,** he created panic by blowing furiously on a conch shell. He was the protector of shepherds and flocks but spent most of his time seducing nymphs or napping.

PANDORA Human beings were warmed by the gods' fire because of **Prometheus,** so a vengeful **Zeus** decided they should have some trouble, too. He asked the Olympians to create Pandora, the first woman, and to make her beautiful but foolish and untrustworthy. Once on Earth, Pandora was forbidden to look in a certain jar. She could not resist and pried open the lid. All the evils in the world swooped out. Pandora snapped the lid shut, saving only hope in the jar.

PARIS The son of King **Priam** and Queen Hecuba was banished at birth. A prophet had said the child would cause the fall of Troy— which he did. Paris eloped with **Helen,** the wife of the king of Sparta. This sparked the Trojan War. Ten war-torn years later, Troy was a smoldering ruin.

PEGASUS When **Perseus** chopped off **Medusa's** head, this beautiful white, winged horse sprang out. **Athena** caught and tamed the magic animal and lent its golden bridle to **Bellerophon.** Pegasus later lived on Olympus and, when commanded, brought **Zeus** his thunderbolt.

PENELOPE Although she had to wait ten long years, this queen was sure her husband, **Odysseus,** would return from the Trojan War. She was surrounded by brutish admirers who insisted she was a widow. Penelope refused to marry any of them until she finished weaving her father-in-law's shroud. Each night, while the palace slept, the grieving queen tore out the threads of her day's work.

PERSEPHONE She became the unhappy and unwilling queen of **Hades.** This beautiful daughter of **Zeus** and **Demeter** was picking flowers when the earth split and Hades flew out on his chariot, drawn by snorting black horses. He seized the maiden and took her down to the underworld to be his wife. Demeter sent cold and famine all over the earth in revenge. Zeus intervened. Hades agreed to free the girl as long she had not eaten any food of the dead. Unfortunately, Persephone had swallowed a pomegranate seed. She had to spend several months each year in Hades, which caused winter upon the earth. When she returned to her mother each spring, plants grew and flowered in celebration.

PERSEUS His father, **Zeus,** seduced his mother, Danae, disguised as a beautiful shower of gold. Their son grew up to be a bold, brave hero who did not shirk from a deadly task: to kill the Gorgon **Medusa.** Perseus borrowed **Hermes'** swift-winged sandals and **Hades'** helmet of invisibility. To avoid being turned to stone by the Gorgon's gaze, he

used his polished shield as a mirror and then chopped off her head. As he flew home, he rescued and then married **Andromeda.**

PHAETON This mortal asked one favor of his immortal father, **Helios,** the sun god: to drive his fiery chariot across the sky. Phaeton couldn't control the charging horses. The sun chariot reeled too high and too low, freezing and scorching the earth. Zeus shot the poor boy out of the sky with a thunderbolt.

POLYDEUCES Often called by his Roman name, Pollux; see **Castor.**

POSEIDON One of the 12 Olympians, this god of the sea, horses, and earthquakes ruled from his golden underwater palace and traveled in a chariot pulled by sea horses. When he shook his mighty trident, the ocean waters roiled and the earth rumbled. His powers were second only to those of his brother, **Zeus.**

PRIAM This kind, just king of Troy was punished by the deeds of his father and of his son. His father had angered **Poseidon** by not paying the god for helping build the great walls of Troy. The sea god vowed to see Troy destroyed. Priam's son **Paris** set the destruction in motion when he abducted **Helen.** When his other son, **Hector,** was killed, the king himself went to beg for the return of the unburied body. **Achilles** was so moved by the noble old king that he agreed. When Troy fell, Priam was slain by Achilles' son.

Poseidon's anger turned **Odysseus's** trip home into a ten-year adventure. He was the only one of his fleet to survive the journey, which included visits to:

- *Lotophagi,* the land of the luscious lotus-fruit, whose taste would make you want to stay there forever.
- *Sicily,* home of the **Cyclopes.**
- *Aeolus,* god of the winds, who gave Odysseus a bag of winds, which his curious crew opened, unleashing terrific storms.
- *Laaestrygonia,* whose cannibal inhabitants destroyed all but Odysseus's own ship.
- *Aeaea,* where the sorceress **Circe** worked her spells.
- The *Sirens,* and *Scylla* and *Charybdis.*
- *Thrinaci,* where some of Odysseus's men foolishly killed the sun god's ox.
- *Calypso,* where the **nymph** charmed Odysseus into staying for several years.

❧

Priam's daughter, the Trojan prophetess Cassandra, could tell the future—but no one believed her. Her powers came from **Apollo,** but when she refused his love, he turned those powers against her. During the Trojan War, Cassandra warned that the Greeks were hiding in the huge wooden horse. The Trojans ignored her, which doomed them to defeat.

Prometheus warned his son Deucalion that **Zeus** was furious with mortals because of their bad behavior. The god planned to flood the entire earth. Like Noah, Deucalion and his wife, Pyrrha, built an ark. They floated in it for nine days and were among the few humans left alive. Zeus told them to walk and throw their mother's bones behind them. The couple was mystified until they realized he meant stones, the "bones" of Mother Earth. When they did the god's bidding, a new race of human beings sprang up.

∾

▼ *This famous gilded bronze sculpture,* Prometheus *by Paul Manship (1885–1966, American) was unveiled in Rockefeller Center, New York City, in 1934.*

PROMETHEUS

He was a **Titan** who sided with **Zeus,** yet defied him to protect human beings. When he created the rituals of animal sacrifice, he tricked Zeus into accepting bones and fat as his share, leaving the meat for people. Then he stole fire from the gods and brought it down to Earth in a fennel stalk, so people could cook and stay warm. Zeus punished Prometheus, first by sending **Pandora** to mortals, then by chaining the Titan to a rock where every day an eagle tore out his liver and every night it grew back because he was immortal.

PSYCHE

Her name means "soul," and her love for her husband, the god **Eros,** was deep, even though he spent only the nights with his mortal wife and told her never to look upon him. Psyche's curiosity won out. She gazed at Eros sleeping, but spilled candle wax on him. The god fled, and Psyche was doomed to performing dangerous, impossible tasks for his jealous mother, **Aphrodite,** before winning back Eros.

SCYLLA AND CHARYBDIS

One side of the Strait of Messina was the whirlpool Charybdis. It could suck in an entire boat. The other side was the monster Scylla. She was once a beautiful **nymph.** Thanks to **Circe,** she was now a horrid, hungry beast with six snarling heads and gnashing teeth. **Jason** and **Odysseus** were among those who sailed through these dire straits.

SIRENS

No one who heard these half-bird, half-woman creatures could resist them. Their bewitching songs lured sailors to their death. Lucky for the **Argonauts, Orpheus** drowned them out with his lyre music; and clever **Odysseus** had his crew plug their ears with wax and tie him to the mast. Both ships passed by safely.

SISYPHUS

This Corinthian king was punished by **Zeus** for telling a river god that the great Olympian had abducted his daughter. He spent eternity in **Hades,** rolling a huge boulder uphill, only to have it roll right back down again.

TANTALUS

The gods were generous to this king and son of **Zeus,** including him in Olympian feasts of ambrosia and nectar. He repaid the gods with his own banquet invitation, where he tested their divine knowledge by killing, boiling, and serving his own son Pelops as the main dish. The gods were wise to his trick and damned

▶ *A Roman mosaic, 1st to 3rd century, inspired by the Greek hero **Theseus** killing the Minotaur, the bull-headed monster.*

Tantalus to **Hades.** He stood in water up to his neck with the branches of a fruit tree dangling over his head. Whenever the thirsty, starving king bent down or reached up the food and water receded.

THESEUS Athens' greatest hero proved he was a prince by lifting a huge stone. Underneath it were a sword and sandals left there by his father, King Aegus. Theseus traveled to Athens, ridding the countryside of outlaws as he went. He was reunited with his father, then volunteered to join the Athenians being sacrificed to the Minotaur in Crete. King **Minos**'s daughter, Ariadne, fell in love with Theseus and helped him slay the Minotaur. She gave him a magic ball of thread that unwound itself through the intricate labyrinth. After killing the monster, Theseus escaped by rewinding the thread. He fled with Ariadne, whom he later abandoned on Naxos. When he sailed into Athens, Theseus forgot to change his black sail to white. His father thought this meant he had been killed. King Aegus jumped into the sea in despair. Theseus became king. Under him, Athens became a united *polis*, or city-state.

TITANS The first offspring of the sky, **Uranus,** and the earth, **Gaia,** was a race of giants who lost control of the universe in the ten-year war with the Olympians.

URANUS The primeval sky god was the passionate lover of **Gaia,** the earth, but Uranus feared their children, so he trapped them inside Gaia. She grew increasingly uncomfortable and finally asked their son **Cronus** to free his siblings.

ZEUS Storm clouds. Rain. Lightning. Thunderbolts. When the lord of the sky was angry, mortals and immortals quaked. Zeus overthrew his father, **Cronus,** and ruled the universe, including Olympus. He was a just god who settled many disputes between his fellow Olympians or on behalf of mortals. He was also a passionate lover. Many Greek myths tell of the wily tricks and clever disguises Zeus used to seduce goddesses, **nymphs,** and women and deceive his goddess wife, **Hera.**

The Greeks honored the gods with sacrifices, temple worship, and festivals. One of the most important of these festivals was the Olympic Games, which were staged in honor of Zeus. They began around 776 B.C.E. and were held every four years at the sanctuary of Zeus in Olympia. (The temple there housed a 40-foot-high statue of the god, *seated*! It was one of the seven wonders of the ancient world.) At Delphi, the Pythian games were held in **Apollo**'s honor. Greece's finest athletes competed in chariot races, running, jumping, javelin throwing, and other contests at these forerunners of the present-day Olympics.

ROME

All roads lead to Rome.

—TRADITIONAL

The Romans had the same attitude about creating a pantheon as they did about conquering a country: absorb and Romanize. They fused their ancient myths with the myths of the Etruscans to the north and the Greeks, Egyptians, and Persians to the south and east. And their hybrid myths not only honored the gods but glorified (and justified!) the Roman Republic and Empire.

Early Roman myths were more about ideas than identity. Roman spirits, called *numen*, were associated with specific activities, from plowing to marrying. The numina didn't really have personalities, stories, or even many temples—until Rome met Greece.

Greek art, myths, and literature were appreciated by the Romans, and the most important Roman gods and goddesses were clearly connected to the Olympians. Other Roman deities, such as Saturn (Cronus) and Faunus (Pan), also had Greek origins.

Some gods, such as Janus, were uniquely Roman, while others, such as Cybele, were imported. The Romans also worshiped many different local gods and even foreign gods. Both the Egyptian goddess Isis and the Persian god Mithra had strong Roman cults.

Myth, History, or Both?

The Romans not only renamed the Greek pantheon, they also redirected its myths. They were used to recreate Rome's history; to explain Roman society; and to reinforce its rules, rites, and customs.

According to legend, Rome was founded in 753 B.C.E. by Romulus and Remus. Seven centuries later, the powerful Romans had conquered all of the lands surrounding the Mediterranean Sea. The Romans wanted a history as grandly heroic as themselves. So they traced their origins all the way back to Aeneas, the warrior of Troy who survived the Trojan War. Romulus and Remus were considered his descendants. And so began the glory of Rome.

Gods and Genii

Romans honored many deities, from Jupiter, the almighty god who headed the powerful Roman pantheon, to *genius*, the spirit of each man who headed a household. Mars, the god of war, and Vesta, goddess of the hearth and guardian of Rome, were especially important to this nation of soldiers and farmers.

Public worship took place in Roman temples built to honor a particular god or goddess. Private worship took place in the *lararium*, a shrine set up in every Roman household.

In keeping with their tradition of mixing myth, history, and politics, the Romans also had state cults, although *pontifices*, or priests, conducted most of those rites. When Rome shifted from being a republic to an empire (c. 27 B.C.E.), many of its emperors were made gods when they died. They, too, required temple worship. The state *lares* had to be honored to keep the nation safe. And there were numerous festivals that were celebrated according to sacred Roman calendars.

Opposite: The Roman Forum, Rome, Italy

▲ *This fresco is from a household shrine, or* lararium, *in Pompeii. The genius of the father of the household was often honored at the home altar.*

At the *lararium*, the family made daily offerings to the *lares, penates,* and *genii,* the spirits that protected the household. The *lares* watched over wealth and property boundaries. The *penates* guarded the cupboard or larder. The *genii* were the essential spirits of a person, place, or thing. A man's genius (or woman's *juno*) was there at birth and died along with him (or her).

AENEAS The goddess Juno stirred up storms, sent Aeneas into **Dido's** arms, and riled up other hostilities all along the way. She did not want Aeneas to achieve his destiny: to found a new empire. But Aeneas had allies. The warrior's mother, Venus, pleaded with Jupiter on her son's behalf. The spirit of his mortal father, Anchises, revealed all his glorious descendants. Aeneas defeated his enemies, married the Latin princess Lavinia, and founded the mighty Roman race. Virgil (70–19 B.C.E.) sang his praises in the famous epic, *Aeneid.*

CYBELE Drums beat. Cymbals clashed. Dancers shouted, bowed, and whirled before her lion-drawn chariot. This powerful fertility goddess was originally worshiped in Asia Minor. In 204 B.C.E., her cult was adopted in Rome on the advice of the Sibylline Books and the oracle of Delphi. The Romans honored her as the Great Mother Goddess but eventually forbade participation in the wild ceremonies held by Cybele's followers.

DIDO After her husband was killed, this beautiful Tyrian queen fled to Africa. There she asked for as much land as she could enclose with an animal hide. Then she cut the hide into strips and spread them widely apart. Everything in between was hers. Dido founded the great city of Carthage, which became Rome's mightiest foe. She fell madly in love with **Aeneas.** When he abandoned her, Dido threw herself onto an enormous funeral pyre.

JANUS The Roman god of beginnings lent his name to what became the first month of our calendar year. Janus is the two-faced god. One looks forward, one looks back. His name comes from *ianua,* the Latin for door, so all doors, gates, and passageways came under his protection. His gateway on the northeast side of the Roman Forum was closed during peacetime. When the Romans threw open Janus's gate, it meant war!

ROMULUS AND REMUS

Their mother, Rhea Silvia, was a vestal virgin who had been raped by the god Mars. When these twins were born, they were tossed into the Tiber River to die. They floated to fame instead. Their small boat washed ashore, and a she-wolf fed the newborns. A shepherd rescued and raised the twins, who became natural leaders. They decided to found a city but quarreled over where it should be. Romulus slew Remus; the city became Rome. Plenty of men but not enough women settled in the new city, so Romulus invited the neighboring Sabines to a celebration. The Romans then drove away the men and kidnapped the Sabine women. Jupiter had to step in before peace was restored. After that, Romulus ruled and Rome flourished. At the end of 40 years, he disappeared in a cloud, only to return declaring himself now a god, Quirinius.

SIBYL OF CUMAE

The stone walls of the oracular cave echoed when the centuries-old prophetess deep within foretold the future. She used her powers to guide **Aeneas.** On her advice, he found and chopped off a magic golden bough that he could use to return from his visit to the underworld. The Sibyl was his guide on the harrowing trip. She also appeared to an Etruscan king, offering to sell him nine books. Each time he refused her price, she burned a few of the volumes. When there were only three books left, the king gave in (at the original price!). He opened the Sibylline Books and found the entire destiny of Rome. The books were closely guarded; only the Roman Senate could order them to be opened.

VESTA

Goddess of the hearth. Protector of Rome. Fires in her honor were kept ever burning in private homes and in Vesta's temple in the Roman Forum. The vestal virgins were the keepers of the eternal flame there. These young maidens entered the goddess's service as young girls. They kept the job for 30 years. They had to keep the fire lit, perform sacred duties, and remain virgins (or be buried alive for being unchaste).

The Roman Pantheon and the Greek Olympians (in parentheses):

- Jupiter (Zeus), king of the gods
- Juno (Hera), queen of the gods
- Mars (Ares), god of war
- Vesta (Hestia), goddess of the hearth
- Apollo (Apollo), god of light, the arts, prophecy
- Bacchus (Dionysus), god of wine and fertility
- Ceres (Demeter), goddess of agriculture
- Cupid (Eros), god of love
- Diana (Artemis), goddess of the hunt
- Mercury (Hermes), messenger of the gods
- Minerva (Athena), goddess of wisdom and crafts
- Neptune (Poseidon), god of the sea
- Pluto/Dis (Hades), god of the underworld
- Venus (Aphrodite), goddess of love
- Vulcan (Hephaestus), god of fire and the forge

◄ *Alexander Calder's (1898–1976, American) whimsical wire sculpture* Romulus and Remus *shows the wolf that nurtured the twins and saved their lives. This animal was sacred to Mars.*

CELTIC LANDS

Truth was in our hearts, strength in our arms, and fulfillment in our tongues.
—THE COLLOQUY OF OLD MEN, The *Fenian Cycle*

Magic weapons. Legendary battles. Undefeated champions, divine and mortal. When the ancient Celts spread out across the European continent and crossed the waters to Great Britain and Ireland, they brought their poetic, heroic traditions with them.

The Celts were not a nation but a combination of peoples who spoke related languages. They probably first emerged in what is now Austria around 800 B.C.E., during the Iron Age. Celtic tribes migrated as far east as Asia Minor and as far west as Ireland. They even once sacked Rome (387 B.C.E.).

Memory vs. Manuscripts

To the Celts, eloquence was as powerful and desirable a trait as strength. But the ancient Celtic peoples believed in memory rather than manuscripts. They did not write down their fabulous stories, myths, and rituals but instead relied on their priestly Druids to share them orally. Europe's "continental Celts" left few traces of their gods and religion. Most of what is known comes from accounts by their Roman conquerors, who usually described the Celtic gods in terms of their own pantheon.

The "insular Celts," the ones who settled in Britain, Wales, Scotland, and Ireland, proved a better source. Even though all those areas, except Ireland, were also conquered by the Romans, mythologies from the insular Celts survived. In the Middle Ages, many ancient (and popular) Irish, Welsh, and British stories were preserved in manuscripts.

The Great Myth Cycles

Most Celtic myths are included within several famous collections. All of them have more than one version; their stories predate their written forms; and some myths influenced others of a different Celtic group.

The famous Irish myth cycles may have first been transcribed in the 8th century. The staunch hero Cuchulainn is at the center of the *Ulster Cycle*, which includes an epic poem. The prose and verse of the *Fenian Cycle* deals with the bold, brash warrior Finn mac Cool and his band of gallant Fenians. The *Mythological Cycle* describes a romantic history of Ireland full of magic, invasions, and the battles of the divine Tuatha de Danaan. The histories of legendary and real Irish rulers form the *Cycle of the Kings*. And many ancient oral Welsh myths were written down in the mid-12th century as *The Four Branches of the Mabinogi*.

Perhaps the most enduring and popular Celtic myths are the ones about King Arthur and the Knights of the Round Table. Many Arthurian legends and characters are based on traditional Welsh and Irish myths. King Arthur himself may have existed as a 6th-century warrior leader in Britain.

Christianity had a great effect on Celtic mythology. Ancient stories were recorded by literate monks in monasteries. Celtic deities were linked to Christian saints. Some myths, especially voyage stories, were seen as Christian allegories. And the search for the Holy Grail became the centerpiece of Arthurian legend.

Opposite: Dun Farvagh, Inishmaan, Ireland

There are many sites in Great Britain sacred in the legends of King Arthur. Legend says it all began at Tintagel Castle in Cornwall, where Arthur was conceived through the trickery of **Merlin**. The original Round Table was once thought to hang in Winchester Castle. Its shape gave all knights sitting around it equal status. Camelot is claimed to have been at Glastonbury, and the Glastonbury Tor (hill) is supposed to hold the tombs of King Arthur and **Guinevere** or hide the entrance to Avalon.

ANGUS   The Irish god of love and youth was born after his father, **Dagda,** seduced a water goddess. He shielded the runaway lovers Grainne and Diarmuid with his cloak of invisibility. His true love was a swan princess. To marry her, the god had to find her in a flock of 150 swans.

ARTHUR   A mysterious arm once rose out of a lake and handed this legendary king his most formidable weapon: Excalibur, the undefeatable sword. King Arthur united Britain, married Queen **Guinevere**, and ruled wisely from his royal court at Camelot. **Merlin** the magician was his adviser. His closest allies were Knights of the Round Table, among them **Lancelot, Gawain, Galahad,** and Perceval. Their skills, valor, and chivalry were unmatched. But while the king and his knights were away conquering the Continent, Arthur's nephew, Mordred, stole the throne. King Arthur returned and killed the usurper but was fatally wounded himself. A mystical boat spirited the king away to the immortal western land, Avalon. The "king that was, king that shall be" will supposedly return at Britain's direst hour of need.

BALOR   It took four servants to lift the heavy eyelid of this cyclops—and one glance from him was fatal. The Irish god of death headed the Fomori, the grotesque sea gods who fought the **Tuatha de Danaan.** He was later blinded and killed by his own grandson, **Lugh.**

BRAN   This voyager hero set sail after finding a magic silver bough. Its owner, a mysterious beauty, sang to him of all the wonders beyond the sea. Bran and his men spent a year visiting the Island of Joy, a place of laughter, and the Island of Women, a place of love and luxury. But when the crew returned home, no one recognized them. So many years had passed that Bran had become an ancient legend.

THE LADY OF THE LAKE TELLETH ARTHVR OF THE SWORD EXCALIBVR

◄ *He was a knight's page, running to find a new sword for his master, when he spotted a fine one embedded in a large stone. Young Arthur took hold and pulled it out—and was crowned king of Britain. This 19th-century book illustration by Aubrey Beardsley (English 1872–1898) shows the Lady of the Lake with **Arthur** (center) and **Merlin** (right).*

❧

Thomas Malory's Morte d'Arthur (1485) and the 12th-century French romances of Chrétien de Troyes are some of the richest sources of stories about wise King Arthur, the chivalrous Knights of the Round Table, and the search for the Holy Grail.

❧

Perceval was one of the most innocent of King **Arthur**'s Knights of the Round Table. He was also one of the few to see the Holy Grail. The would-be knight rode out of his remote forest home to Camelot on a bony old horse, carrying sharpened sticks instead of a sword. Once knighted, Perceval later discovered the mystical castle of the crippled Fisher King, guardian of the grail. He saw a dazzling procession and a beautiful woman holding a jeweled golden grail. Perceval unknowingly failed to ask "Whom does the grail serve?" and the vision disappeared.

BRAN THE BLESSED No boat could hold this gigantic son of the Welsh sea god **Lir.** When he invaded Ireland, he strode through the sea alongside his fleet. Bran's sister Branwen, wife of the Irish king, was unfairly mistreated and asked for her brother's help. His army was victorious, but Bran was killed. He had his men cut off his head and take it home for burial. It was a long trip. They stopped at an enchanted palace and were entertained by Bran's head, which could still merrily eat and talk. The feast lasted 80 years. The spell was broken when one man opened a palace door, saw the real world, and remembered their promise. Bran's head was buried in London, facing east to ward off future invaders.

BRIGID The number three was very important in Celtic myth, and there were actually three Brigids, all daughters of **Dagda.** One was the Irish goddess of learning, wisdom, and poetry; one was expert in the art of healing and fertility; and the third protected craft and metalworkers. However, they were all often referred to as a singular Brigid or Brigit.

CERNUNNOS He's cross-legged and crowned with magnificent stag horns, as befitting a god whose name means the Horned One. Widely worshipped as the Celtic god of animals, the hunt, and fertility, his cult actually predates the Celts.

CORMAC MAC AIRT According to legend, this king of Ireland was born in a thunderstorm and nursed by a wolf. He ruled from Tara, the seat of the kings, and was close to **Finn mac Cool.** Many myths from the Irish Fenian Cycle took place during his reign (c. 227–266), a period of great abundance.

The Celts were a rugged, energetic people who generally lived in fortified compounds called *duns* or *raths*. They were renowned ironworkers and irrepressible adventurers. A good Celtic myth always involves fighting, honor, love, or a quest, complicated further by oaths and obligation or magic and enchantment.

❧

A statue, *Death of Cuchulainn*, stands in the General Post Office in Dublin, Ireland, site of the 1916 Easter Rising, a famous battle for Irish independence. The bronze statue shows **Cuchulainn** stalwartly dying on his feet and is a memorial to those involved in the struggle to establish the Republic of Ireland.

❧

▶ *Bloody, pierced by spears, bruised by blows,* **Cuchulainn** *refused to fall in his final battle. He lashed himself to a stone pillar and died on his feet. Still, his enemies didn't dare approach his body until three days later, when* Morrigan, *the goddess of war, flew down as a crow and settled on the corpse's shoulder.*

CUCHULAINN   It was clear when this Irish warrior was ready for battle. His hair stood on end. One eye sank into his head and the other became a big, red, bulging orb. His foaming mouth spread from ear to ear, and a column of blood shot out of his head. Cuchulainn is the son of **Lugh,** who spirited away a **Druid's** daughter from her own wedding and impregnated her with their warrior offspring. As a boy, he was so strong he killed a lunging hound with his bare hands and earned his name, which means Hound of Culann. He single-handedly defended Ulster against Queen **Medb's** forces in the famous Cattle Raid of Cooley. Medb became his bitterest enemy along with Morrigan, goddess of war, whose love Cuchulainn had rashly spurned, and three sorcerer daughters of a warrior he had killed. Their magic and betrayal brought a madness upon Cuchulainn, and he was mortally wounded with his own spear.

DAGDA   This chieftain of the **Tuatha de Danaan** had an incredible appetite for food and battle, but his name also means the Good. So while one end of his double-edged club slew nine men at a time, the other brought them back to life. The Tuatha's foes, the Fomori, once forced Dagda, on pain of death, to empty a hole filled with a porridge of whole

animals. He picked up a ladle big enough to hold a man and woman and drained the hole.

DANA   She is the ancient Celtic mother goddess whom the Irish called Anu and the Welsh named Don. Her divine children are the **Tuatha de Danann.**

DEIRDRE   "Among the chariot men of Ulster/She will cause great slaughter." This prediction about the Irish beauty and tragic heroine of the Ulster Cycle proved too true. Wooed by old King Conchobar mac Nessa, Deirdre eloped with young, handsome Naoise. They lived in exile until the king tricked them into coming back. Many, including Naoise, were slain in a treacherous plot. His heartbroken widow bent her head with grief and never lifted it off her knee for a year. Conchobar, in a rage, gave her to Naoise's murderer. Deirdre leaped from his chariot and killed herself.

DIAN CECHT Dead or wounded warriors who were plunged in his magic springs were restored. The Irish god of medicine also crafted a beautiful silver arm for **Nuadhu** when his was cut off in battle. But Dian Cecht was a jealous god. He mixed up his daughter's careful catalog of healing herbs and killed his son who had outshone him by making a real arm for Nuadhu.

DRUIDS It could take 20 years of training to gain the wisdom of these Celtic priests and priestesses. They presided over rituals and sacrifices. They practiced divination and healing. They memorized the sacred stories and were moral and legal authorities. Many famous Druids appear in Celtic myths.

EPONA Her name means great mare, and she is usually shown riding a steed sidesaddle. This widely worshiped Celtic goddess of horses and fertility was also popular with Roman soldiers.

FINN MAC COOL/FIONN MAC CUMHAILL He led the finest band of warriors in Ireland, the Fianna. To join, a man had to pass many difficult tests, such as reciting 12 books of poetry or standing in a waist-high pit armed only with a shield and letting nine men throw their spears—without getting a single wound. Finn and his Fianna defended the kings of Ireland against all foes, natural and supernatural. They were also keen hunters. When they hunted the magic boar of Ben Bulben, Finn finally was avenged on Diarmuid, a fellow warrior who had run off with Finn's betrothed, Grainne. Diarmuid was mortally wounded by the boar. Water from Finn's healing hands could save him, but when Finn remembered Grainne, he let the water trickle away.

▲ *There are many important cauldrons in Celtic mythology.* **Dagda's** *cauldron never ran empty of delicious food. The divine Welsh king of Britain,* **Bran the Blessed,** *had a cauldron in which the dead were dipped and brought back to life, although they couldn't talk. This silver Gundestrup cauldron (c. 2nd century B.C.E.), found in a Danish peat bog, is one of the most famous pieces of Celtic religious art. Shown is* **Cernunnos,** *holding a torc, or divine neck ring, and a serpent, possibly a symbol of renewal.*

When he was a boy, **Finn mac Cool** cooked the Salmon of Knowledge for his **Druid** tutor, who told him not to eat any of it. Finn burned his thumb, licked the blister, and was blessed with wisdom. Finn grew into a visionary warrior and hunter. His spear never missed—and if he needed to know something, he just sucked his thumb to find out.

∾

Doomed love and passionate lovers are popular themes in Celtic mythology. Irish **Deirdre** and her husband, Naoise, lived the life of fugitives. So did Diarmuid, the foster son of **Angus,** and Grainne, the daughter of **Cormac mac Airt.** She was betrothed to an aging **Finn mac Cool** but insisted that Diarmuid run away with her. The legendary Tristan and Iseult also inspired many romances, poems, and operas. He was a Knight of the Round Table. She was an Irish princess married to Tristan's uncle. The two unwittingly drank a love potion together to disastrous and deadly effect.

GALAHAD This knight came to the Round Table and sat in the Siege Perilous, the only empty chair. All others who dared the same had been swallowed up by the earth. This was the sign that Galahad, son of **Lancelot** and purest and humblest of all knights, would find the Holy Grail. After many adventures, Galahad did find the sacred relic. He was so transfixed that he lost all desire to live. A host of angels carried him to heaven—and a hand came down and bore off the grail. It was never seen again.

GAWAIN A huge green knight strode into King **Arthur**'s court at Camelot, and the perfect knight, Gawain, didn't shrink from his challenge: a beheading contest. With one whack, Gawain severed the stranger's head. The green giant picked it up, tucked it under his arm, and told Gawain to meet him in a year. Then it would be the giant's turn. A year later, Gawain knelt before the giant but flinched before the green knight's ax met his neck. Gawain was spared, but he

was also less perfect. A similar but earlier story was told about **Cuchulainn** (who held steady).

GUINEVERE The Round Table split apart because of this beautiful Queen of Camelot. When King **Arthur** learned of his beloved wife's adulterous affair with **Lancelot,** he declared war on the fallen knight. The other knights were forced to choose allegiances. The queen was to be burned at the stake, but Lancelot heroically rescued her. The lovers were never reunited. Guinevere became a nun, Lancelot a hermit.

LANCELOT The greatest knight of the Round Table was also Camelot's most tragic. Handsome, brave, chivalrous, Lancelot was hopelessly in love with King **Arthur**'s wife, **Guinevere.** Every joust, battle, tournament he engaged in was for her honor. The two became lovers, which not only divided the Round Table but destroyed Lancelot's chances of ever obtaining the Holy Grail. Only the pure could do so, but because of his courage, Lancelot was allowed a brief look at the holy vessel. When he moved toward the grail, he was knocked to the ground, and he lay in a trance for 24 days.

LIR The Irish sea god is the father of **Manannan.** His second wife turned his four children into swans. By the time he was able to save them, they had grown old. The Welsh call him Llyr.

LUGH His grandfather, **Balor,** was evil. His son, **Cuchulainn,** was heroic. And this handsome Irish sun god was the master of all arts. He could forge and wield weapons, play the harp, recite poetry, and beat anyone at fidchell, a popular chesslike game some myths say he invented. Lugh helped **Nuadhu** and the **Tuatha de Danaan** in their pitched battle against the monstrous Fomori. Using a magic stone and a slingshot, he hit Balor so hard that his lethal eye was pushed out the back of his head, and its deadly gaze killed all the Fomori troops behind him.

MAEL DUIN This Irish voyager set out to find his father's killers. What he and his crew found first were 31 incredible islands. Each had its own pleasures, dangers, or curiosities. The sailors reveled in a lake of eternal youth, ate from an orchard of intoxicating fruit, and drank from a fountain of beer. But they were also beset by a colony of ants as big as horses and wild beasts with sharp-nailed hooves.

MANANNAN A son of **Lir,** this Irish sea god traveled his watery kingdom in a self-sailing boat, the Wave Sweeper, or in a horse-drawn chariot that rode the waves as if they were land. He wore a flaming helmet, an impenetrable breastplate, and a magic cape of invisibility that also changed colors. A great magician, Manannan gave **Cormac mac Airt** a golden cup that shattered at lies and a musical silver apple bough that cured the sick. The Welsh called him Manawydan.

▼ *The Holy Grail was believed to be the cup Jesus Christ used at the Last Supper and the one that was filled with blood from a spear wound at his crucifixion. This painting by Dante Gabriel Rossetti (1828–1882, English), How Sir Galahad, Sir Bors and Sir Percival were Fed with the Sanc Grael (1864), shows its restorative powers. The Christian Holy Grail links to the more ancient Celtic stories about magic cauldrons.*

The Celts loved fantastic voyages. Stories and epics about long, time-warped journeys to other worlds were very popular. The seafaring exploits of heroes like **Bran** and **Mael Duin** probably influenced the stories told about St. Brendan the Navigator. This 6th-century Irish monk first sailed in a little curragh, a small boat made of tarred leather hides. He was looking for the Land of Promise revealed to him in a vision. According to legend, he encountered whales, giants, enormous animals, and volcanoes. According to history, Irish monks probably reached Iceland, though there are claims that St. Brendan sailed as far as Newfoundland, Canada.

▶ Morgan Le Fay by A.F.A. Sandys (1829–1904, English). A certain mirage seen at sea is called fata morgana because people believed the enchantress causes it with her sorcery.

MEDB The wild Irish Queen of Connacht was irate that her husband was wealthier than she—by one bull. Even worse, the king's White-horned One had been hers, but the bull refused to stay in a herd owned by a woman. Medb went after its twin, the Brown Bull of Cuailgne. Plans to borrow the bull from its owner went awry, so the queen staged a cattle raid. The retaliatory battle pitted Medb's Men of Ireland against the Men of Ulster, whose mightiest warrior was **Cuchulainn.** When the Ulster hero insisted on single combat, Medb connived to have his foster father and then his friend fight against him. Cuchulainn defeated all of Queen Medb's forces. The bulls locked horns and rampaged their way across the country.

MERLIN Celtic mythology's most famous magician and seer was only half mortal. His father was an incubus, or devil. Merlin's wizardry is at the heart of many Arthurian legends, including King **Arthur**'s very conception. Merlin raised the child and created the legendary sword in the stone that proved Arthur's claim to the throne. He served as King Arthur's adviser and built the Round Table for his court. The great wizard was ultimately betrayed by his treacherous mistress and disappeared.

MORGAN LE FAY She could fly on wings, change shape, and cast spells. This beautiful sorceress was King **Arthur**'s half sister. She often schemed against her famous sibling but accompanied his body on the mystical boat trip to Avalon.

NUADHU This Irish god and leader of the **Tuatha de Danaan** lost his arm in the battle against the Firbolgs. **Dian Cecht** replaced it with a silver arm, but only the "unblemished" could be king. The tyrannical Bres ruled in his stead until Dian Cecht's son made Nuadhu a new arm of flesh. Nuadhu remained king until he abdicated to the greater power of **Lugh.**

OGMIOS The Celtic god of eloquence spoke so sweetly that he was often shown as a bald old man with a group of happy listeners, their ears chained to his tongue. The Irish called him Oghma, the inventor of their ancient alphabet. Often carved on stones, oghma used lines and notches to represent letters.

OISIN In the Fenian Cycle of myths, this son of **Finn mac Cool** tells St. Patrick, patron saint of Ireland, all about the exploits of Finn's Fenians. Oisin also traveled with a fairy to live happily in Tir na nOg, the Land of Eternal Youth. Eventually the poet warrior missed Ireland. The fairy gave him her magic white steed but warned him never to dismount. Oisin's saddle slipped. He hit the ground, the horse disappeared, and Oisin became a blind old man. He'd really been gone for 300 years.

PRYDERI Like his father, **Pwyll,** this beloved Welsh king sat on a legendary magic mound—but no vision appeared. Instead, his kingdom became a wasteland, his subjects, animals, and wealth vanished. Only his wife, his mother, Rhiannon, and her second husband, Manawydan (or **Manannan**), remained. One day a wild boar lured Pryderi into a mysterious castle. He entered, drank from a gold cup, and froze, mute. So did Rhiannon, who followed him. The castle disappeared in a mist. Manawydan forced the enchanter, an enemy of Pwyll's, to release them by holding the enchanter's wife hostage. She had shape-shifted into a little gray mouse in order to eat Manawydan's corn.

PWYLL This Welsh chieftain saw a stag and tried to exchange his dogs for the pack that had brought the animal down. But those fierce red-eyed dogs belonged to Arawn, god of the underworld. Pwyll was forced to change places with the

god for one year. During this time, he had to defeat Arawn's fierce enemy and share his beautiful wife's bed but not make love to her. Pwyll valiantly succeeded.

TUATHA DE DANAAN The people of the goddess **Dana** were the last divine beings to rule Ireland. They had treasures such as a spear and a sword that never failed, a cooking cauldron that was never empty, and a stone that cried out when a rightful king of Ireland stepped on it. Their rule was a peaceful golden age that ended when they were defeated by the Milesians, the mortal ancestors of the Irish people. The Tuatha de Danaan retired to splendid underground kingdoms and became identified with the *sidhe*, the Irish fairies.

◄ The Beguiling of Merlin *by Edward Burne-Jones (1833–1898, English) shows him at the mercy of his beautiful mistress. Nimuë convinced the infatuated wizard to teach her his magic, which she then used to imprison him in an oak tree, a tower, a cave, or a mist.*

❧

Anyone who sat on a certain magic mound would suddenly be beaten or bedazzled. King **Pwyll** sat down. He was overcome by a vision of a beautiful woman dressed in gold brocade. She rode a horse that no one could overtake. Pwyll shouted out his love and Rhiannon halted. She was his future wife. Later, Pwyll unjustly accused Rhiannon of murdering and eating their newborn, **Pryderi.** The Welsh queen's dreadful sentence was to stand outside the castle for seven years and offer to give all callers a ride in on her back. The child reappeared after his kidnapping by a rival suitor. Rhiannon is often linked to the horse goddess **Epona.**

NORSE LANDS

Further in the future afar I behold,
The twilight of the gods who gave victory.

—FROM "THE SONG OF SIBYL," *The Poetic Edda*

Geography greatly influenced mythology in northern, central, and eastern Europe. In the forbidding, glacial North, the Norse culture produced Viking myths as fierce and rugged as these "fighting men."

Vikings Set Sail

In the 3rd century, some Germanic tribes moved north into Scandinavia (Denmark, Norway, and Sweden). These Northmen, or Norse, became the Vikings, the fierce, seafaring conquerors who, between 780 and 1070, raided and sacked European coastal towns; sailed to North America; and migrated east to Russia and west to Greenland, the British Isles, and most important, Iceland.

Medieval Icelandic literature is key to understanding Norse mythology. The Norse themselves shared their myths orally. They left no written records, although they carved stone markers with mythic details and symbols. The Icelandic scholar Snorri Sturluson (1179–1241) wrote down many Norse myths about gods, giants, dwarfs, magic animals, and amazing weapons in *The Prose Edda*.

From Chaos to Catastrophe

Viking gods weren't the first Scandinavian gods. Bronze Age people (1600–450 B.C.E.) left rock carvings that show gods, goddesses, animal masks, and sacred ships. But it's the heroic, violent myths of the Norse that became famous.

The Vikings lived in a world that was harsh and dangerous. Their mythical world was just as threatening. Aesir, or sky gods, fought Vanir, earth gods. Giants were always lurking. A violent end of the world was inevitable. Even Odin and Thor, the most powerful gods, were doomed.

In the Norse cosmos, Yggdrasil, the World Tree, supported nine worlds. The highest realm was Asgard, the splendid home of Odin and the other Aesir. Midgard, the middle world of mortals, was connected to the gods' home by the rainbow bridge Bifrost. A frightening world serpent, Jormungard, encircled Midgard by biting its own tail. Giants or *jotun* lived in the tree's roots and personified cataclysmic forces like volcanoes or earthquakes. A magic spring bubbled at the tree's foot. The Norse gods held their councils there; so did the three shadowy Norns, Fate, Being, and Necessity, who decided the future of every god and person born.

Norse myths start in chaos and end in catastrophe. The Vikings believed that the world began as a void, Ginnungagap. Then Niflheim, the frozen land, melted under the scorching heat of Muspell, the fire land. A giant and a cow were born of the thaw. Ymir produced more frost giants. Audumla licked the ancestor of the gods from the ice. The god Odin and his brothers killed the primeval giant and used his body to create the world. The bloody battle lines were drawn.

The gods, especially Thor, defended themselves against the giants in all kinds of heroic adventures. But in the end, gods and giants would clash at one last, violent battle, Ragnarok. All would be destroyed—and the whole world would go up in flames.

Opposite: Viking memorial stone, Gotland Island, Sweden

The sky gods wanted to keep frost ogres and giants out of their divine home Asgard. A mysterious stranger promised to build them a thick, high wall. In exchange, he wanted the sun, the moon—and **Freya.** The Aesir were appalled at losing all their light sources and their beautiful goddess. **Loki** talked them into the deal but set impossible conditions: The builder could only use his horse as a helper, and the job had to be done over one winter. At winter's end, the wall was nearly finished, and the gods were frantic. They turned on Loki. He changed into a mare and distracted the builder's stallion. The builder turned out to be a giant, so **Thor** raised his mighty hammer against him. Several months later, Loki bore a magic foal. It was the swift, eight-legged steed, **Sleipnir.**

❧

▶ *In* The Prose Edda, *Snorri Sturluson called* **Balder**'s *death "the greatest misfortune ever to befall gods and men." Balder's body was burned in a funeral pyre aboard a ship so big the gods could not launch it. They summoned an ogress from the land of the giants to help them. Viking warriors were often buried or burned in their long ships along with food, armor, and other treasures.*

ANDVARI Under severe and painful threats from **Loki,** this goldsmith gave up the **dwarfs'** treasure, including his own fabulous ring. The ring could create more and more wealth. Loki seized it eagerly, but not before Andvari put a curse on the ring's owners forever. **Fafnir** and **Sigurd** later found out how powerful and fatal that curse truly was.

ASKR AND EMBLA Two pieces of beach driftwood were the raw materials of human life in one Norse creation myth. **Odin** breathed onto an ash tree lying in the sand. The bark split, and the first man, Askr, emerged. He did the same to an elm tree, and when the bark rolled back, the first woman, Embla, was revealed. Odin's brothers then gave the couple movement, senses, and speech.

AUDUMLA When the heat of Muspell thawed the frost of Niflheim, this first cow was born. Four rivers of milk gushed from her udders and fed the first frost giant, **Ymir.** The hungry cow then began to lick the salty ice blocks all around her. Her warm saliva melted more frost, and a crown of hair appeared. Another day of licking and a male head emerged; by the third day Audumla nuzzled out the first god, Buri, whose grandson was **Odin.**

BALDER Beautiful. Good. Beloved by the gods, especially his parents **Odin** and **Frigg,** this Norse deity dreamed of his own death. His frightened mother made all things in the world vow not to hurt him. After that, the gods playfully tossed stones or spears at their invincible favorite. **Loki** grew terribly jealous. He disguised himself as an old woman and wheedled Frigg into telling him the secret of Balder's strength. Then he used this information to trick **Hoder** into killing Balder. The death of Balder and the loss of all the goodness he represented set the world on its inevitable, doomed course toward **Ragnarok.**

BRYNHILD Though one of the immortal **Valkyries,** she was condemned, for disobeying **Odin,** to marry a mortal. The great god clad the beauty in armor and put her inside a blazing ring of fire. Brynhild was to lay there, sleeping, until the first man came along—no matter how old, ugly, or mean. Luckily, the noble **Sigurd** came to her rescue. Unluckily, through spells and trickery, the two lovers were parted. Brynhild later revealed Sigurd's one vulnerable spot and brought about his death. She leaped onto his funeral pyre in remorse.

DWARFS Maggots crawled out of **Ymir**'s flesh and became these small, bearded, industrious creatures. Most of the *dvergar* lived in rocks, mountains, or caves. They were skilled metalworkers who forged beautiful magic objects like **Odin**'s spear, Gungnir, and his ring, Draupnir; **Thor**'s hammer, Mjollnir; **Frey**'s golden boar; and **Freya**'s necklace.

FAFNIR This greedy son stole his father's treasure, including **Andvari**'s cursed gold ring. He shape-shifted into a fire-breathing dragon and coiled up on his hoard. Fafnir's brother, the skilled smithy Regin, wanted his fair share of the loot, so he appealed to **Sigurd** for help. On **Odin**'s secret advice, Sigurd crouched in a pit over which Fafnir slithered on his way to a water hole. With one thrust from below, he pierced the dragon's heart, bathed in Fafnir's blood, and became invincible, except for a spot that went unwashed.

FENRIR This giant wolf grew so menacing that even the gods feared him. The offspring of **Loki**, Fenrir was raised in Asgard. The gods didn't want to kill something in their sacred abode, so they decided to chain the fierce wolf instead. Twice the gods tricked Fenrir into a noose, but all he had to do was stretch, and the chains shattered. Finally the gods asked the **dwarfs**

for a magic chain that couldn't be broken. Suspicious, Fenrir refused the noose until a god put his hand in his mouth as a sign that the chain was harmless. **Tyr** was the only god bold enough to do it.

FREY Along with his twin, **Freya**, this Vanir god of peace and prosperity was widely worshiped. He was linked with the sun because his boar, Goldenbristle, traveled across the sky and disappeared under the earth. Frey himself sometimes rode in a boar-drawn chariot, galloped on his horse that traveled through fire and over water, or sailed on his magic boat, *Skidbladnir*. This ship was big enough to hold all the gods but still neatly folded up into a pouch.

▲ *This illustration of* **Brynhild** *by Arthur Rackham (1867–1939, British) was for Richard Wagner's* The Rhinegold *and the* Valkyrie.

❧

The chain that would bind **Fenrir** had to be invincible, so the **dwarfs** forged it out of things that were invisible: the roots of a mountain, the sound of a cat's paw, the spittle of a bird, the sinews of a bear, the breath of a fish, and the beard of a woman. The dwarfs' silky strand bound the sinister wolf to a rock until the destruction of Ragnarok.

▶ *When **Freya** threw on her magic feather cloak, she could fly like a falcon. She also had a cat-drawn chariot, and sometimes she rode a cat herself.*

～

The giantess Skadi was outraged when her father, Thjazi, was killed over **Idunn**'s apples. She donned her armor and weapons and went after the gods. To appease her, they offered her one of them as a husband. But they were afraid she would choose the sweet, handsome **Balder**, so Skadi was only allowed to see the gods' feet before choosing. She picked the most beautiful pair—which belonged to **Njord**. His feet had been washed smooth and white by the sea.

～

Mistletoe, the plant used to kill **Balder**, was also sacred to the Celts. Celtic Druids cut it down with a golden sickle to use in rituals.

FREYA Daughter of **Njord**, twin sister of **Frey**, and ruler of the Vanir, this beautiful goddess of love and fertility was often sought in marriage by giants. She had many divine lovers, and when she wanted a particularly beautiful gold necklace, she agreed to sleep one night with each of the **dwarfs** who had crafted it. Freya is sometimes also called the head of the **Valkyries** and is said to take half of the heroes slain in battle to her magnificent hall. The other half go to **Valhalla.**

FRIGG The queen of the Aesir and the wife of **Odin** is a stately sky goddess. She lived in her own palace; her weaving turned into clouds, her robes turned the colors of the sky. Frigg is the protector of marriage and children but was unable to save her own son, **Balder.** Frigg had asked all things, gods, humans, animals, plants, even rocks and minerals not to harm her son. But she overlooked the lowly mistletoe—with fatal consequences.

GERDA This giantess was so beautiful that when she raised her arms the sky and sea brightened. Her brilliant light also attracted **Frey**'s attention. The god had secretly climbed up onto **Odin**'s throne for a glimpse of the wide world. Now he was hopelessly lovesick. Gerda refused to marry Frey unless he gave the giants his magic sword, which could fight on its own. The god finally gave in, which left him fatally unarmed at **Ragnarok.**

HEIMDALL Silently the "white god" stands guardian at the edge of Bifrost to keep the giants from crossing this rainbow bridge to Asgard. Ever vigilant, he can see in the dark and even hear grass grow.

HEL Half of her is fleshy and female; the other half is black, putrid, and rotting. This hideous daughter of **Loki** rules the land of the dead from her frigid palace, Sleetcold. Her table is set with the knife and fork of famine and the plate of hunger. People who died from disease or old age entered her kingdom.

HERMOD When **Balder,** his brother, was slain, Hermod leaped upon **Sleipnir** and fearlessly raced the eight-legged beast to the land of the dead. There he begged **Hel** to return his brother to the living. She agreed—provided all things in heaven and on Earth wept for the dead god. The very stones shed tears. Only **Loki,** disguised as an old hag, refused: "Let Hel hold what she has." So she did.

HODER This blind god couldn't even see the dart with which he unwittingly killed his twin. But evil guided his hand. The spiteful god **Loki** convinced Hoder to playfully throw a piece of mistletoe at his brother **Balder**. Loki knew the small plant was the only living thing that could harm the beloved god.

IDUNN The Norse gods were always glad to see this divine maiden. Each day she handed out their golden apples of immortality. **Loki** lured her out of Asgard because he was beholden to a giant, Thjazi. The giant turned into an eagle and snatched Idunn and her apples. The gods grew wrinkled and gray. They threatened to kill Loki. The trickster god flew off as a falcon to look for Idunn. When he found her, he changed her into a nut and carried her back to Asgard in his beak. When the giant eagle gave chase, the other gods set a fire and burned him out of the sky.

LOKI This famous trickster god was so sly the Norse called him the Father of Lies. Loki was conceived when his father, a giant, shot a fireball at his mother, a shrubby island, which linked the god to fire and lightning. Loki was handsome, entertaining, shifty eyed, and cunning, all at once. And he could shape-shift at will. To the other gods, Loki was both problem and solution. He would stir up trouble, and then use his wiles to help the gods. He often traveled with **Odin** or **Thor** on their adventures but also sired the monsters that would destroy them at the end of the world. The gods had had enough

Thor got his magic hammer because **Loki** cut off his wife Sif's hair. Thor threatened to kill the trickster. Loki bought his freedom by promising to get the **dwarfs** to make magic presents for the gods. Loki got some dwarfs to forge new golden hair for Sif; **Odin's** spear that never misses; and **Frey's** foldable boat. Loki bragged to other rival dwarfs that they could have his head (and only that) if they could make finer objects. These dwarfs made a gold boar that came alive; Odin's ring that every ninth night produces eight other rings, and Thor's deadly hammer that could smash anything. Loki got worried about the bet and turned himself into a fly. He hoped his stings would ruin the working dwarfs' concentration. In the end, the gods decided that the hammer was the finest treasure because it could smite giants. The dwarfs tried to collect Loki's head—but the crafty god reminded them that he'd wagered only his head, not the neck they'd have to cut to get it.

❧

◄ *The head of Loki is carved on this Viking furnace or forge stone.*

▲ *Every day **Odin** sent his two ravens, Huginn (Thought) and Munnin (Memory), out flying. They brought back all the news of the Norse worlds.*

❧

Odin once stabbed himself with a spear and then hung himself on Yggdrasil, the sacred ash Tree of Life, for nine agonizing days and nights. After this sacrifice, he knew the secrets of the runes, the alphabetic Norse symbols whose wisdom and magic he shared with people.

after Loki caused **Balder**'s death and prevented his resurrection. They shackled him to a rock underneath a venom-dripping serpent. His wife caught the liquid, but each time she left to empty the bowl, the burning poison fell into Loki's eyes. His painful writhing caused earthquakes.

MIMIR One of the few good giants, Mimir guards the spring of wisdom, which bubbles under a root of the Tree of Life. **Odin** had to give him an eye for a single drink of the magic water. The Vanir chopped off Mimir's head when he was their hostage. Odin preserved the head in herbs and set it among Yggdrasil's roots, where it drank from the spring every day. Whenever Odin needed advice, he went down to consult Mimir.

NJORD The sea god who rules the Vanir is also the father of **Frey** and **Freya.** He protected ships, sailors, and fishing, which were an important part of Norse life. Njord was married to a giantess, Skadi, but the two did not live together. He could not abide the howling wolves of her mountain home, and she could not stand the screeching seagulls in his kingdom.

ODIN He brought glory to heroes on the battlefield and inspiration to poets. He ruled Asgard with wisdom that was hard-won. Odin, the All-Father, the mysterious god of death, is the most powerful of all the Norse gods. He could defend anything with his spear that never missed and be generous with his magic ring that reproduced itself. Odin forfeited an eye for one sip from **Mimir**'s spring of wisdom. Because he could then tell the future, he often visited humans. Disguised as a one-eyed old man, half hidden in a large cloak and a broad-brimmed hat, the god always had some magic weapon or advice to share. In his greatest sacrifice, Odin hung himself from Yggdrasil to learn the mysteries of the runes. In his legendary hall, **Valhalla,** the brave dead await the final battle, **Ragnarok.** Gold-helmeted Odin will lead the charge.

RAGNAROK A wolf will swallow the sun. An earthquake will shatter **Fenrir**'s chains. The world serpent Jormungard will spew out poisonous fumes and cause a tidal wave. **Loki, Hel,** and their vile crew will set sail on the boat of the dead. **Heimdall,** the watchman, will blow his great horn, the golden cock will crow, and all in Asgard will know—the Twilight of the Gods has finally arrived. The Norse had an elaborate vision of the end of the world where the gods and giants clashed and everything was lost in a fiery blaze. All of their major deities were destroyed and even Yggdrasil, the Tree of Life, shook. However, the sons of **Odin** and **Thor** and a human man and woman clung to its branches and were saved. In time, a rich, new Earth will arise, just as **Balder** will arise from the dead and join the sons of the gods in this new, beautiful world.

SIGURD The young prince made a serious mistake after he slew **Fafnir** with the magic sword **Odin** had given to his father. Sigurd took **Andvari**'s cursed gold ring from the evil dragon's treasure pile. He betrothed himself to the **Valkyrie Brynhild** with this ring. But a magic love potion erased his memory, and he was tricked into marrying Gudrun. Sigurd, disguised as his brother-in-law, rescued Brynhild a second time and took back the fatal ring. Tragedy followed, and both of them died.

SKRYMIR This giant is so huge that **Thor** and his companions slept in the thumb of his glove, thinking it was a vast hall. The giant's snoring woke the gods. Thor leaped up and hit him with his magic hammer. The giant just yawned and asked if an acorn had fallen on his head. Skrymir was actually King **Utgard-Loki** in disguise.

The Romans named the days of the week after their gods. The Germanic peoples (which includes the Norse) did the same thing. Tiw's day (**Tyr**), Woden's day (**Odin**), **Thor**'s day, and **Frigg**'s day gave us Tuesday, Wednesday, Thursday, and Friday.

◄ *". . . a wind age, a wolf age/before the world's ruin."* That's how *The Prose Edda* described the onset of **Ragnarok**. In the terrible battle, **Fenrir** will devour **Odin**, but his son will tear open the jaws of the vicious wolf and shove a sword down to his very heart. **Thor** and Jormungard will lock in fierce combat; the god will slay the world serpent with his hammer but then fall dead from poisonous venom. Fatal violence will overtake all the gods. The world will be engulfed in cataclysmic flames. Even the stars will fall.*

Thor, disguised as a boy, once went fishing with a sea giant, Hyrmir. The giant told him to get some bait, so the god cut off the head of Hyrmir's prize ox. He told him to row, so Thor churned the waters so rapidly with his oar that they reached the realm of the world serpent. He tossed the ox head in, and Jormungard snatched it between his deadly jaws. Thor stood and reeled the fishing line in so forcefully that his feet crashed through the boat to the ocean floor. Jormungard writhed and snapped at the god. Just as Thor raised his mighty hammer to kill the monster, Hyrmir cut the line in terror. Thor's hammer came crashing down on him in retaliation. Jormungard dove back into the deep.

❧

▶ *There are many myths about* **Thor** *and his powerful weapons. When he threw his hammer, Mjollnir (the Destroyer or Crusher), it killed on contact and then flew back into the god's hand. It was so powerful he needed iron gauntlets to hold it. These gloves could also shatter rocks, and with his magic belt Thor could double his size and strength. The Norse wore replicas of Thor's hammer as protective amulets and also carved it on stone markers.*

SLEIPNIR Eight legs and a divine father make him the fastest horse in any Norse world. Born of **Loki,** this gray stallion could charge into battle, gallop among the clouds, or travel through the land of the dead. Sleipnir was the mount of **Odin.**

SURT For eons, he has guarded the entrance to Muspell. But at the end of the world, this fiery giant will brandish his sword that's hotter than the sun and lead his army of giants into the raging battle of **Ragnarok.** Bifrost, the rainbow bridge to Asgard, will shatter under the pounding of their horses' hooves.

THOR Big, burly, red-headed with a full beard and blazing eyes. This Norse god of thunder looked as powerful as he was. Strongest of the gods, Thor was fearless and took on all kinds of enemies, from giants

like **Thrym** and **Utgard-Loki** to the world serpent, Jormungard. He rode across the heavens in a chariot driven by his two goats, Toothgnasher and Toothgrinder. When he raised his hammer, thunder rumbled; when he dashed it to the earth, lightning struck. Thor was the greatest champion of the gods against their eternal enemies, the giants.

THRYM When this giant stole **Thor**'s hammer, his asking price for its return was **Freya**'s hand in marriage. **Loki** dressed Thor up as the goddess, and they went off to the wedding feast. Thrym was astonished at his bride's appetite. She swilled gallons of mead and swallowed a whole ox and lots of salmon. The giant king was alarmed by her flashing red eyes. Loki told him this was all just excitement at the marriage. So Thrym followed custom: He put a hammer in the bride's lap. Thor gripped his mighty weapon, threw off his veil, and slew everyone at the feast.

TYR This Norse war god ruled over battles and sorted out matters of law and order. He was eventually replaced in the Norse hierarchy by the more powerful **Odin.** However, Tyr is an important figure in one myth. He was the only god fearless enough to go near the wolf **Fenrir**—which cost him his hand.

UTGARD-LOKI Disguised as **Skrymir,** this giant king led **Thor** and his companions to his kingdom. Utgard-Loki then challenged the gods to several contests of strength. All Thor had to do was empty a drinking horn, lift the king's cat, and wrestle an old woman. But the undefeatable god was full after three sips, only got the cat to lift a paw, and was brought down to one knee by the granny. Utgard-Loki then revealed his magic: The bottom of the drinking horn was hidden in the ocean, which even Thor couldn't drain. The cat was really the world serpent Jormungard. And the woman was Old Age, whom even mighty Thor could not defeat.

VALHALLA

This Hall of the Slain had 640 doors, each of which could be thrown open to 960 warriors standing side by side. Its golden roof was made from warriors' shields; its torchlit walls rang with the sound of feasting and fighting. Here **Odin** reigned supreme over the those who had valiantly fought and died and been brought to his hall by the **Valkyries.** Every day, the heroes trained for the ultimate battle with the giants; every night they drank and feasted.

VALKYRIES

At **Odin**'s command, these supernatural beauties donned their shining armor and charged into battles on their magnificent horses. They determined who lived and who died by the sword that day. The Valkyries were invisible to the living, but when the bravest, most heroic fighters died, they were borne up on the Valkyries' mounts to **Valhalla.** There the immortal warrior women served horns of sacred beer and mead.

YMIR

The primeval thaw of Niflheim formed this hoary, sleeping giant. The hot air of Muspell made him sweat. A giant man and woman came out from under his damp armpit. His feet mated and produced a monstrous, six-headed frost giant. All three terrible giants reproduced until **Odin** and his brothers later slew Ymir. A deluge of blood drowned all the giants except one, whose descendants were ever after the enemies of the gods. Meanwhile, Odin and the others hacked up Ymir's body to create the mortal world called Midgard. They stretched his skin to make the ground, spread his bones and teeth to make mountains and rocks, and used his hair for vegetation. Ymir's flowing blood became the sea. The gods tossed his brains up to make clouds, hoisted up his skull to make the sky, and ordered four **dwarfs** to hold its corners high. Finally, they wrapped Ymir's eyebrows around Midgard, making a thick wall to keep out any giants.

▲ *Myths and historical accounts about bold, brave Viking adventurers and heroes inspired art like this painting,* Discovery of America. *It is by an unknown painter of the 19th-century American School art tradition.*

〜

Richard Wagner (1813–1883, German) wrote the opera *The Ride of the Valkyries* as part of his four-opera cycle, *Der Ring des Nibelungen* (*The Ring Cycle*). It is based on Norse and Germanic myths, including the story of **Brynhild** and **Sigurd.** The stirring operatic piece of music that signals the arrival of the **Valkyries** is very famous.

NORTH AMERICA

Every part of this country is sacred to my people.
— CHIEF SEATHL OF THE DWAMISH, *This Beautiful Land* (1854)

From the Northwest fishers to the Southeast farmers, the mythology of Native Americans is deeply tied to the land. Though only several hundred tribes exist today, there once were as many as 2,000 tribes spread across what is now the United States and Canada. Each tribe had its own rich religion and spiritual myths, so the only way to reasonably approach such diversity is through geography.

Tribal mythology is often discussed in terms of cultural areas, like the Northwest (for example, the Clayoquot, Haida, Kwakiutl, Quinault, and Tlingit peoples), the West (Maidu, Modoc), the Southwest (Hopi, Navajo, Zuni), the Plateau and Basin (Nez Percé, Paiute, Shoshone, Wishram), the Plains (Blackfoot, Lakota, Omaha, Pawnee), the Southeast (Cherokee, Creek), the Northeast (Iroquois, Algonquin, Huron, Selish), and the Arctic (Inuit). There were many communities within each area, but there are some beliefs that were common to all and remain an important part of many Native Americans' lives today.

Spirits and Shamans

To Native Americans, the supernatural world has a tremendous impact on the natural world. There is a spirit quality to all things in the natural world. Spirits can be protective or destructive, but they are always active in people's lives. Contact with these spirits is not only desirable, it is essential for the well-being of the community and for a deeper understanding of the world.

Shamans have the most powerful access to the spirit world. These wise men explore the meanings and messages of the supernatural world. They invoke spirits at tribal ceremonies or dances, where sacred myths are reenacted and mythic rituals celebrated.

First Gods, First People

Most Native Americans believe in a Great Spirit, a creator god who made the world or set the process in motion. He is sometimes described as an all-encompassing mystery. Great Spirit, who goes by many names, often had help from deities like Sky Father, Earth Mother, and animal gods who finished forming the world.

Many creation myths assume that animals were the world's first inhabitants. They were large, behaved like people, and could even remove their fur. Lots of myths feature an Earth Diver. This animal dived into the primeval waters and brought up the mud that grew into the earth, often on top of a turtle's back.

Many tribes believe that the world is multilevel: earth in the middle; good or sky spirits are in the world above; monsters or enemies are below. Some Native Americans have complicated origin myths about how their ancestors climbed up through several lower worlds, often guided by a hero or helped by animals. In hero myths, this revered guide taught people all the social and survival skills they needed. In trickster myths, wily animals brought people useful things like sunlight or fire—and darker things like death.

Opposite: Totem pole, Sitka National Park, Alaska

Shamans are the tribal intermediaries between the spirit and the natural worlds. They often go into trances when contacting or being contacted by spirits. Because of their great spiritual knowledge and power, shamans are also great healers.

Members of a tribe also went through spiritual training. Young boys, and sometimes girls, were sent on vision quests as they reached puberty. They spent time in the wilderness alone, praying for visits from the spirit who would be their life guardian.

❧

▶ *False faces were evil spirits that appeared as supernatural flying heads. Iroquois shamans belonged to the False Face Society. They wore grotesque masks, danced noisily, and shook turtle rattles while chanting to scare off the evil spirits.*

AMOTKEN   The creator god of the Selish made three worlds: heaven, earth, and the underworld, which were supported by a giant pillar. He plucked five hairs from his head and they became women. The wise old god asked them what they wanted to be, and that's how the mothers of earth, fire, water, goodness, and evil were created. Amotken retired to live alone in heaven.

ATANENSIC   According to Iroquois and Huron creation myths, this Sky Woman fell through a hole in the sky. The Great Turtle urged all the water animals to dive into the ocean and get mud to put on his back. Muskrat succeeded, and the soil expanded into a island that broke Atanensic's fall. She or her daughter later gave birth to the twins **Hahgwehdiyr and Hahgwehdaetgah.**

AWONAWILONA   The supreme being of the Zuni existed before all else and was both male and female. The primeval mist that warmed to an ocean came from this creator god's thoughts and warmth. Eventually Mother Earth and Father Sky formed, and from them all living things grew in four wombs. Divine twins built a living ladder out of trees and vines so the animals and first humans could make the difficult climb up to the earth. The first humans were strange, scaly black creatures with enormous ears, owl eyes, webbed feet, and short tails. The first great Zuni priest, Yanualuha, taught them all of the civilized ways of their new life.

COYOTE   This wily trickster god is both crafty and comic and brought the world good things and bad. In one story, Coyote killed a monster that had swallowed all the world's animal people. But in another, he introduces death to the world **Wonomi** created. Old man Coyote stole summer from the crone who kept it captive in a bag while people shuddered through long cold winters. But he distracted another creator who was baking clay into the first humans. Some people were undercooked and some burned, which is why people are different colors. Coyote stole fire for people but also stole a water monster's children. The monster caused a world deluge. Another time, he kidnapped the spirits of the dead to bring them back to the world. But Coyote tired of carrying them in a heavy basket. When he put it down, the spirits escaped, and the trickster wearily decreed that human death would be final. Coyote is an important character in many myths and legends of the Southwest, West, and Plains area people.

ESTSANATLEHI Navajo creator spirits, the Yei, created this beloved earth goddess from turquoise and her sister Yolkai Estan from white shells. Estsanatlehi grew up in 18 days and ever after aged in winter, only to become young again in the spring. She created men and women by mixing dust from her breasts with cornmeal and water. Estsanatlehi also gave birth to the heroes **Nayenezgani and Tobadzistsini.** Then she retired to her floating lodge in the western waters, where every night the sun god **Tsohanoai** visits her. She is revered for sending the rains, snow, and growing seasons.

GLOOSKAP AND MALSUM The divine creator twins of the Algonquin were complete opposites. Glooskap sent something beautiful into the world; his wolf brother, Malsum, subverted it. One twin made fertile plains, the other rocky mountains. Glooskap made food plants and animals; Malsum made poisonous ones. His jealous evil brother finally shot Glooskap with an owl feather, the only thing to which he was vulnerable. But he was resurrected, killed his wolf brother with a fern,

and went on creating the world. When he was finished, Glooskap sailed off in a birch-bark canoe, someday to return.

HAHGWEHDIYR AND HAHGWEHDAETGAH Also called Yoskeha (Sapling) and Taswiscana (Flint), these creator twins of the Iroquois represent the forces of good and evil. Flint was so obstreperous he burst out of his mother's armpit and killed her. Sapling, the good god, made his mother's face the sun and used parts of her body to make a fertile earth. Flint besieged his brother's creation with earthquakes and hurricanes. He added thorns to Sapling's fruits, bones to his edible fish, and made monsters when the good god created people. Flint was eventually defeated by his brother and banished, most myths say to the underworld.

▲ *This 19th-century Navajo blanket is based on traditional sand painting design. It shows sacred figures flanking a corn plant. Sand paintings are sacred ceremonial art that must be exactly executed according to traditional designs. After the ritual, the paintings are destroyed.*

❧

Corn was the most important crop to most Native Americans. The Navajo believe their creator sent White Corn Boy and Yellow Corn Girl with the first ears. In other myths, a Corn Maiden or a grandmother secretly rubbed the kernels off her body. People spied on her and were repulsed. The woman then sacrificed herself; corn plants grew from her grave.

Many tribes of the Great Plains held an annual sun dance to celebrate the sun's role in the earth's renewal and prosperity. The complex ceremony lasted several days and included fasting, feasting, and a ritualistic sun dance. A special tree was chopped down, painted and decorated, and raised as a symbolic link to the worlds above and below the earth. Warriors who sought the sun's spiritual power danced around this central pole, following the path of the sun across the sky. They were often skewered through the chest and attached by ropes to the pole. Physical pain was seen as a spiritual release and a sacred offering.

▶ *Kachina*
fetishes are given to young children to study so they will be prepared for the sacred rituals that are held from January until July. Kachina ceremonies celebrate the spirits' powers to bring rain and prosperity.

HAIO HWA THA (HIAWATHA)

This legendary Iroquois hero united the rival Mohawk, Onondaga, Seneca, Oneida, and Cayuga into the fraternal League of Nations. But he had to overcome a formidable foe first. Atotarho (Thadodaho) was a powerful Onondaga shaman. His gaze could kill; his hair writhed with serpents because of his evil anger. Hiawatha finally convinced Atotarho to support the league.

Then the hero took a carved bone comb and cleaned the snakes out of the shaman's hair to ease his mind. Henry Wadsworth Longfellow (1807–1882, American) wrote a famous poem called *The Song of Hiawatha* that is based on Algonquin myths.

KACHINAS Misty rain clouds signal their presence; several months of masked dances celebrate their arrival. Kachinas are the essential spirits of Pueblo peoples of the Southwest, especially the Hopi and Zuni. They represent as many as 500 different spirits: ancestors, animals, agricultural, and most important, rain. Elaborately carved and painted masks are used in kachina rituals, which include traditional dances and even tomfoolery from clown kachinas.

KUMUSH The Old Man of the Ancients was lonely in the world he'd created, so he and his daughters traveled to the underworld. He gathered a big basket of spirit bones but fell twice, and the spirits jumped out singing and sped back to the underworld. On the third try, Kumush made it up the steep slope, tossed the basket onto the earth, and yelled "Indian bones." The Modoc say this is how the first people came forth from the bones.

NANABOZHO This Great Hare helped the Algonquin great spirit, Kici Manitou, with creation. He showed people how to make fire, fish, and set traps. He taught the animals how to protect themselves. When his second brother was drowned by enemies, Nanabozho forced them to reveal their sacred healing and medicine secrets, which he then shared with people. He is also a trickster god.

NAPI The wise old man creator god of the Blackfoot made the world by rolling mud balls that a muskrat retrieved from the primal waters. The mud balls expanded into the earth, which a wolf ran across and shaped into mountains, plains, lakes, and rivers. Napi then molded people from clay. A woman asked if they would live forever. Napi threw a piece of wood into a river. He said that if it floated, dead people would breathe again after four days. The wood floated. A woman tossed a stone in and said that if it floated there would be no death at all. The stone sank. Death became permanent.

NAYENEZGANI AND TOBADZISTSINI Giants and monster animals were no match for these twin Navajo warrior gods. The Blessed Two protected the world from evil. They beheaded a giant who threw 400 thunderbolts at them. Tobadzistsini then tilled the earth, while Nayenezgani roamed it, looking for danger. He burrowed under a flesh-eating deer beast and shot an arrow through its heart. He was captured in the talons of a huge carnivorous bird but slew it with his thunderbolts. He also dispatched an ogre who kicked people off mountains, and a race of evil ones who killed by shooting lightning from their eyes. But a few foes did survive the twin's battles: hunger, poverty, cold, and old age.

RAVEN Creator. Trickster. Thief. Raven has many roles in Northwest tribal myths. He was tossed out of heaven and in flapping his wings caused land to rise from the primeval waters. He discovered humans in a clamshell. Or else he called them forth from the ground. He tricked a fisherman's wife into giving him the family's fish and once lost his beak stealing a fisherman's catch. He brought people salmon, berries, and most important, the sun and moon.

SEDNA The great goddess of the Inuit was tossed into the sea by her giant parents. It may be because she ate any flesh she could find, including her sleeping parents' limbs. Or maybe because she married a dog or a bird against their wishes. When Sedna was thrown overboard she clung to

◀ *This Tlingit headdress represents* **Raven**.

the boat. Her father chopped off her fingers, which grew into whales, walruses, seals, and fish. Sedna sank. She rules the underworld and all sea creatures. Storms rage when she is angry.

SPIDER WOMAN This powerful spirit is wise and kind. She helped the Hopi escape the world flood by leading them up several tall plants and finally a sunflower to a safer world. Smoke rising from her underground dwelling attracted the Navajo heroes **Nayenezgani and Tobadzistsini.** She warned them of the four fatal dangers they would face on their journey to the sun god's house: the crushing rocks, the sharp reeds that were like knives, the cactus thorns that shredded flesh, and the boiling sands. Then she gave them four magic feathers to survive these and other ordeals that would be set against them by their father, **Tsohanoai.**

Crafty **Raven** changed into a pine needle, which the Sky Chief's daughter swallowed. This made her pregnant. Her beak-nosed, dark baby was always wailing for his grandfather's possessions. Finally, the Sky Chief let the baby play with a box filled with bright light. The baby transformed into Raven. The bird flew around the world and released sunlight everywhere. Another myth has Raven stealing the moon in the same way.

As in other ancient mythologies, creator twins, warrior twins, or twin rivals representing light and dark forces appear in many different Native American myths. Mythic animals sometimes have counterparts as well.

White Buffalo Calf Woman brought two sacred things: the sacred pipe and the buffalo. She taught the Lakota the prayers and pipe-smoking ceremony that would send their messages to **Wakan Tanka**. As she left, she rolled over four times, becoming a red, black, brown, and finally a white buffalo again. Then she disappeared over the horizon, and just as suddenly a great herd of buffalo appeared.

❧

Many Native Americans, especially Plains people, use calumets or sacred pipes. The pipes are beautifully carved from wood or stone and decorated with symbolic images, including feathers or animal claws. The pipes were used during rituals like the Pipe Dance or the Sun Dance. Smoking tobacco was also believed to encourage peace, so pipes might be smoked or exchanged at inter-tribal meetings or to honor contracts.

❧

▶ *The buffalo was highly revered by Plains peoples because it provided their food, clothing, and shelter. In the buffalo dance, celebrants wear the animal's hide and horns. The ceremony is enacted to give thanks for the buffalo, pray for its survival, and ask for the resurrection of the ones slain for food.*

THUNDERBIRD Lightning sparks from his eyes. Thunder claps from his beating wings. His sharp talons can carry off a whale. Native Americans call this mythical bird by many names, but its role is always the same: to defeat cosmic evil. When Thunderbird fought with underwater monsters like snakes and panthers, the battles caused earthquakes, floods, and storms. One battle created Niagara Falls. Those on vision quests often pray for a visit from this powerful being.

TIRAWA The Pawnee's Great Spirit is the great celestial and world organizer. He put the sun, moon, and stars in place and gave them some of his powers so they could watch over a creation to come: people. He placed a great buffalo to hold up the northwest sky and then had the spirits of the four corners sing the earth into existence. Thunderstorms are his messengers. Tirawa ordered the sun and moon to marry to make the first man; then the morning and evening stars wed to make the first woman.

TSOHANOAI The sun god of the Navajo carries the sun on his back across the sky. When he returns to his beautiful turquoise house, he hangs the burning orb on his western wall. The sun god refused to recognize his sons, **Nayenezgani and Tobadzistsini,** when they came to his house. He tested them by tossing them out onto

sharp mountain peaks, steaming them in a big pot, and forcing them to smoke a pipe of poison. The twins survived and proved themselves warriors. The sun god gave them magic weapons like lightning arrows, thunderbolts, and a wind charm.

WAKAN TANKA The breath of life. The blue of the sky. The wind blowing. The sun burning. The rainbow's colorful hues. Everything in the world has a *wakan*, a spirit. And Wakan Tanka, the supreme being of the Plains tribes, encompasses all these spirits, all the creative power of the universe. To the Lakota, Wakan Tanka, the Great Mystery, was first Inyan (Rock) and Han (Darkness). Inyan grew lonely, so he created Maka (Earth), water, and Skan (Sky). From all their parts, Skan created Wi (Sun). The four elemental gods continued creating until there were 16 divine manifestations, but they were all one in Wakan Tanka.

WAKONDA In the beginning, all things existed in the mind of this powerful deity of the Omaha. All people and animals were originally spirits floating in the cosmos, looking for a place to live. The sun was too hot; the moon was too dark; and the earth was all water. Suddenly, a huge rock arose and burst into flames. The water turned into clouds, land appeared, and the spirits settled on it, becoming flesh-and-blood animals and people. Wakonda is the spirit who inspired and managed this creation.

WISHPOOSH
Beaver was a gigantic, greedy animal who drowned anyone who dared fish in his lake. The starving people prayed to **Coyote** for help. He speared but didn't kill Wishpoosh, who dragged both of them into a downstream river. Their fierce battle changed the entire landscape. Coyote then turned himself into a branch, which Beaver swallowed while gorging on whales. Once inside, the trickster resumed his shape and stabbed Beaver to death. Coyote used Wishpoosh's carcass to create the Nez Percé and other Plateau peoples.

WONOMI The supreme sky god of the Maidu of California created human beings into a world where life was good. There was plenty of food and songs of prayer. There was no sickness or death—until **Coyote** came along. He thought he could improve on creation and make it more interesting. So the trickster introduced disease, sorrow, and death. His own son was the first to die. Coyote had more influence over people, so Wonomi retired to his sky home in the clouds.

▲ *This contemporary sculpture,* Shaman Summoning Sedna *by Abraham Anghik (1951– , Native American), shows an Inuit shaman or* angakoq *beseeching the sea goddess on behalf of his people.*

⤴

At a young age male and female Inuit shamans had to spend time alone in a deserted place, awaiting a visitation from a *tornaq*, his or her guardian spirit. *Angakoqs* held tribal séances where they went into trances to drive out sickness, control the weather, or communicate with the gods. When the Inuit faced food shortages, the shaman sent his or her soul into the great whirlpool that led down to **Sedna's** sea tent.

CENTRAL AMERICA

Let beings appear who will praise us.

—THE MAYAN CREATOR GODS, *Popul Vuh (Book of Advice)*

The mythologies of Mesoamerica, ancient Mexico and Central America, reveal cultures of devotion, duality, and doom. Olmecs, Mayas, Toltecs, and Aztecs based their societies on worship and warding off the catastrophes sure to come if the gods were not honored and fed, usually with human sacrifice. They believed the world had already been destroyed and reborn several times.

Mesoamerica's earliest people, the Olmecs (c. 1200–400 B.C.E.), introduced many of the ideas that influenced the area's later cultures: the astronomical calendars, ceremonial pyramids and plazas, ritualistic ball courts, huge monuments, beautiful jade and stone carvings. Olmec gods were absorbed by the Mayas, Toltecs, and Aztecs who followed.

Magnificent Empires

The magnificent Maya empire stretched over the Yucatán peninsula, Guatemala, Belize, east Campeche, and western Honduras. An ancient culture that may date back to 2600 B.C.E., it flourished from around 300 to 900 C.E.

The Mayas built incredible cities with thousands of massive buildings, many of them stepped pyramids topped with temples. They recorded their history in hieroglyphs and were particularly concerned with time calculation, which was tied into their sacred beliefs.

The Mayas believed a sacred tree ran through the center of a multileveled world. The heavenly sky was at the top; the nine levels of the underworld were at the bottom. Maya creator gods populated the middle world with human beings. They decided to make people who would praise them. The gods' first attempts were failures. Their mud people melted in the rain; their wood people had no spirit or wisdom. Finally, the gods used maize and successfully created the first people.

Violent Ends

Many aspects of Aztec culture were adopted from the Toltecs. The Toltecs came down from the north and established a powerful capital at Tula (near present-day Mexico City) by 950. They embraced the worship of an older god, Quetzalcoatl, and expanded to large-scale human sacrifice. The Aztecs went even further with that religious ritual. They added a warrior sun god with a huge appetite for human blood. Thousands died.

The Aztecs believed that the world had five eras or suns. The first sun was devoured by jaguars. The second sun was blown away by a hurricane and people were turned into monkeys. People turned into birds before the third sun was destroyed by fire; the fourth sun was wiped out with a deluge. The fifth sun, the present age, is due to be destroyed by earthquakes.

Mesoamerica's mythology, like its history, is rich but not always fully understood. When the Spanish conquerors overpowered the indigenous peoples in the 1500s, they destroyed many kinds of architecture and artifacts that would have provided important clues to these ancient myths and their meanings.

Opposite: Temple of the Warriors, Chichén Itzá, Yucatán, Mexico

The Aztecs, like many ancient Central American peoples, believed that their gods needed to be fed—and only human blood would satisfy them. It was particularly important to sacrifice to the sun gods Tonatiuh and **Huitzilopochtli** to ensure that the sun continued its daily journey. Sacrifice might also help ward off the cataclysmic destruction of this world, the fifth sun. So the Aztecs waged flower wars against neighbors and rival city-states. They captured victims to get the blossoming heart and flowers, or blood, they needed for sun rituals. Tens of thousands of people were sacrificed at Tenochtitlán's Great Temple, sometimes in one day. The victims' still-beating hearts were cut out with flint or quartz knives. The heart was ritually burned; the body was thrown down the long temple stairs. Sometimes parts of it were cooked and eaten.

*▶ When **Coatlicue** lost her head, it was replaced by two fanged serpents. This eight-foot-high statue of the Aztec goddess, with her claw feet and necklace of sacrificial hands and hearts, was so terrifying that it was reburied several times after it was found in the early 18th century.*

AH PUCH   The Maya god of death is a hideous sight. He appears as either a bony skeleton or a bloated corpse. Ah Puch rules over nine underworlds. As Hunhua, he is an owl-headed man. The bird's screech means death is taking someone.

CINTEOTL   Many statues show him wearing a headdress made of corncobs. This god protected the Aztecs' most important crop, maize. Another part of him is the corn goddess Chicomecoatl.

COATLICUE   Giving birth was difficult for this Aztec Goddess of the Serpent Petticoat. She became

pregnant after she tucked some white feathers in her breast. Her other children, the moon goddess and 400 star gods, were enraged and attacked her. Coatlicue's head was chopped off, and blue-skinned **Huitzilopochtli** leaped out, fully armed with a shield and spear. Coatlicue is the supreme earth goddess with power over life, death, and the cosmic balance. Her good favors required sacrifice, and she was both worshiped and feared.

EHECATL   The Aztec wind god blew love into the world. He brought the heavenly maiden Mayahuel down to earth, where the two of them entwined and turned into a tree. As a manifestation of **Quetzalcoatl,** the wind god also lured musicians from the House of the Sun to bring beautiful sound to a silent world.

HUITZILOPOCHTLI   He has distinctive blue skin and bird feathers down his left leg. This symbolizes Huitzilopochtli's power as a war god, because warrior souls were thought to change into hummingbirds. But this god was also a powerful sun god and the chief patron of the Aztecs. When the Aztecs migrated south, Huitzilopochtli led the way. He spoke to his people through the sacred medicine bundle his priests carried. The Aztecs dedicated their island capital, Tenochtitlán, to this god. Home of palaces, temples, and a million people, this incredible city was built with canals and floating rafts.

HUNAPU AND XBALANQUE In their most famous adventure, these magician trickster heroes of the ancient Maya text *Popul Vuh* trump the gods of the underworld. The death lords had beheaded their father for making too much noise playing ball, so the twins went down to Xibalba to avenge him. The angry gods threw them into the Shivering House of Cold, but the twins built a fire. The gods tossed them into the House of Jaguars, but the twins threw bones to the beasts and tamed them. Next, the twins were locked in the bat house. They hid in their blowpipes, but Hunapu peeked out, and a monster bat lopped off his head. Xbalanque convinced a turtle to impersonate the missing head, and the brothers then played a fierce ball game with the gods. Through trickery, they stole back the real head and won the games. Next, the twins did their most famous trick: dismembering and reassembling themselves. The gods begged to try this. Hunapu and Xbalanque obliged. They chopped

them to bits but never put the gods back together. Then the heroes went up to heaven to become the sun and the moon.

HURACÁN The blustery god of winds once imprisoned Homshuk, the divine Olmec personification of corn. Homshuk survived the god's three jails of serpents, tigers, and flying arrows. The god eventually recognized Homshuk's importance and promised to keep him watered. The word *hurricane* comes from this deity, who is also one of the Mayas' creator gods.

ITZAMNÁ Unlike his aloof father, Hunab, this god was very active and very present in Maya life. He taught people sacred rituals and skills like writing and the arts. He knew the ways of medicine and agriculture. Itzamná showed people how to raise and use corn, cocoa, and rubber. And though he was the supreme god of heaven, the moon god, and husband of **Ixchel,** he still looked like a little old man with a hooked nose.

▲ *Diego Rivera (1886–1957, Mexican) celebrated Central American myth and culture in his frescoes at the Palacio Nationale in Mexico City. This mural is called* The Great City of Tenochtitlan.

❧

The underworld ball game played by trickster heroes **Hunapu and Xbalanque** was actually a very important ritualistic game. Ball courts stood next to temples throughout Central America. Players had to "shoot" a ball through a hoop on the wall—but without using their hands or feet. The ball was controlled by elbows, hips, and buttocks.

Quetzalcoatl rejected human sacrifice, which angered his eternal enemy, **Tezcatlipoca**. This bloodthirsty god showed the benevolent god his magic smoking mirror. Quetzalcoatl was shocked to see his old, sagging face. Tezcatlipoca dressed him up in a bright, plumed robe and mask. The evil god then tricked the good god into getting so drunk that he slept with his own sister. A remorseful Quetzalcoatl then lay in a stone box for four days. His city was abandoned, his palace burned. The god lit his own funeral pyre and leaped in. Beautiful birds flew out of his ashes.

～

▶ *Some myths say* **Quetzalcoatl** *left the world bedecked in his feathered robe and mask. He sailed off on a raft of serpents. The Aztecs believed he would return one day and destroy everything. According to their complex calendars, that would happen in Aztec year 1 Reed (1519), the same year the Spanish conquistador Hermán Cortés arrived — and the Aztec empire did come to an end.*

IXCHEL Lady Rainbow was married to the great Maya god **Itzamná.** Together they produced the rest of the Maya pantheon— and there may have been 166 gods! Goddess of weaving, medicine, childbirth, and maybe the moon, Ixchel had a vessel filled with floodwaters, which she could overturn if angered.

MICTLANTECUHTLI The Aztec lord of death ruled over Mictlan, a kingdom at the center of the Earth. The trip there was fearsome and involved climbing mountains, crossing deserts, and fighting off beasts. But in Mictlan itself, the dead experienced neither pleasure nor pain. Xochiquetzal ruled the more desirable part of the underworld that was reserved for warriors who died in battle or were sacrificed.

OMECÍHUATL The goddess aspect of **Ometéotl** is the mother of an obsidian knife. After she gave birth to the flint, she flung it down to Earth, where it became 1,600 heroes. They wanted servants, so they sent the dog deity Xolotl down to the underworld to get help.

OMETÉOTL The powerful creator of the universe embodies the very idea of dual natures,

since he is both the Aztec god Ometecuhtli and the goddess **Omecíhuatl.** He stands on the top, thirteenth rung of the heavenly ladder and is lord of everything. The offspring of Ometecuhtli and Omecíhuatl are the four creator gods: **Quetzalcoatl, Tezcatlipoca, Huitzilopochtli,** and **Xipe Totec.**

QUETZALCOATL He is the most widely worshiped, widely depicted of all the Central American gods. This Feathered Serpent is the complex but loving god of all the world's opposites: spirit and matter, heaven and earth, light and dark, life and death. There are several myths about his creation and some that suggest he was once a mortal Toltec king of Tula. Quetzalcoatl brought people learning, laws, and their famous ancient calendar.

TECCIZTECATL The fourth sun of the Aztec world ended, but a divine sacrifice was required to banish darkness and bring the fifth sun into existence. The gods built a roaring fire. Proud Tecciztecatl brought his offerings of gold, jewels, and feathers and prepared to leap into the flames. At the last minute he flinched; a homely god, Nanautzin, jumped in and became the sun. Mortified, Tecciztecatl threw himself into the flames. But the fire had died down, so he became the dimmer moon.

TEZCATLIPOCA In his dark, reflective obsidian disk, this Lord of the Smoking Mirror can see everything, even the future. He is the unruly forces of nature, the pleasures of sin, the jaguar god of the night, the opponent of the benign **Quetzalcoatl**. He is not just one of, but all four of the creator gods. Quetzalcoatl, **Huitzilopochtli**, and **Xipe Totec** were all Tezcatlipocas, differentiated by separate colors and

compass points. He descended from heaven on a spider web and ruled the first Aztec world or sun.

TLALOC He is goggle-eyed and has giant teeth. But as god of rain and water, he was so revered that young children were sacrificed to him. Tlaloc had four jugs of water at his command. One poured out the soft rain plants needed. Blight, frost, and destruction gushed out of each of the other three. Both the Toltecs and the Aztecs worshiped this ancient rain god; the Mayas called him Chac.

XIPE TOTEC The god of spring suffered painfully to bring on the season of growth and vegetation. So did the humans who were skinned alive in his honor. Xipe Totec, through his victims, was flayed. To the Aztecs, this was providential and was like a seed losing its skin in order to grow into a plant. Statues or priests of the flayed god were dressed in the sacrificial skins until they decayed and fell off. This symbolized spring fertility.

▲ *A human skull covered in turquoise represents the Aztec god **Tezcatlipoca**.*

The beloved god **Quetzalcoatl** had a twin: ugly, dog-headed Xolotl. His feet were turned backward, and one eye had burst. Xolotl went down to the underworld to fetch a bone to help the heroes born of **Omecíhuatl/Ometéotl**. He was chased out by the death lord and dropped the bone. Xolotl picked up the bone shards, mixed them with his blood, and created human beings.

SOUTH AMERICA

. . . they showed themselves to be children of the sun . . .

— GARCILASO INCA DE LA VEGA (1540–1616, INCA),
Comentarios Reales de los Incas

When the sun shines on South America, its rays travel over lush rain forests, the peaks of the Andes Mountains, the Pacific coastal lands. Ancient cultures throughout the continent watched and worshiped not only the sun but the moon, the stars, and a whole host of nature deities.

Incredible gold and silver work, imaginatively decorated pottery, elaborate urban and temple ruins, and magical forest rituals are all signs of the rich diversity of South American mythology. But interpreting these signs isn't easy.

Ancient South American peoples were preliterate. None of them had a writing system, so their sacred myths and rituals were passed down orally. Changes in culture or government meant changes in myths. When the Incas started consolidating their vast coastal empire in 1438, they adapted the myths of older cultures like the Nazca, the Mochica, or the Chimu. When the Spanish conquerors came in 1531, they abolished many mythic traditions and plundered many sacred objects. Their chroniclers did write accounts of ancient South American mythology but these were colored by Christian perspectives.

Supernatural Nature

Despite the difficulty in tracing South American myths, there are a few things that seem common to many of the continent's peoples. From jungle cultures to coastal civilizations, almost everyone had a flood myth, a catastrophe from which a new, finer race of human beings emerged.

Artifacts also suggest that most people held some kind of belief in the supernatural power of jaguars or anacondas. Ancestor worship was widespread, and burial rites were often elaborate to ensure that the dead were comfortable in the afterlife.

Tribal people of the Amazon River basin of Brazil, Venezuela, Guyana, Surinam, or French Guiana had many origin and order myths. They believed in a natural world that was filled with the supernatural and lived side by side with all kinds of demons and animal and nature spirits. Like their North American counterparts, shamans protected the welfare of the tribe. They used ritual, magic, and sometimes hallucinatory plants to communicate with the spirit world and interpret visions.

Sun Gods and Mummies

The Inca empire stretched 2,500 miles from northern Ecuador through Peru to central Chile. By the time this advanced civilization reached its peak in the 15th century, it had absorbed many earlier mythic ideas about a supreme creator god, the creation of people, and the importance of the sun god.

The Incas had thousands of priests and handmaidens of the sun who served in their spectacular temples. Great festivals were held, especially on the solstices, and rituals included processions of the mummies of Inca rulers or sacrifices of sacred animals like the white llama—or if times were really bad, humans.

Opposite: Inca ruins, Machu Picchu, Peru

▶ This 11th- or 12th-century gold mask from northern Peru shows a sun god with solar rays tipped with serpents. It is often identified as **Inti** or **Viracocha**. Gold was the most sacred metal to South American peoples, who used it to honor their gods. The search for gold plunder drove the Spanish conquest, especially the story of El Dorado. The king of this mythical city was said to be covered in gold. Powdering a new king with gold dust was actually a practice in the highlands of Columbia. It signified his ascension to the throne.

❧

There are many South American myths about creator gods and first people. The Chibcha believed the mother goddess Bachue married her son and populated the world before they both turned into sea serpents. Omam, creator god of the Yanomami (Amazon), caught the first woman while fishing. Some Peruvian coastal peoples believed the first humans came from gold, silver, and copper eggs. A Brazilian tribe has a myth about the first people tunneling up from underground to steal food from two magicians. These people had tusks and webbed hands and feet, which the magicians changed to teeth, fingers, and toes.

AYARS The first Peruvian ancestors emerged from the middle mouth of a cave with three openings. The four brothers and four sisters wore fine wool and carried gold objects. One of them was so strong and boastful that the others walled him back up in the cave. He turned into a sacred stone. Later he appeared in a vision and sent his siblings to build the great Inca city of Cuzco. It was ruled by an Ayar brother and sister couple, **Manco Capac and Mama Ocollo.**

BOCHICA Sometimes the chief god of the Chibcha was invisible. Sometimes he was a bearded old man who appeared, bringing with him all civilized law and knowledge. He saved people from a deluge caused by his wife Chie, the moon goddess, and the earth god Chibchacum. Bochica rode a rainbow, shattered a mountain, and

the flood drained off as a waterfall. Chie was banished to the night sky. Chibchacum was forced to hold up the world. Earthquakes occur when he shifts shoulders.

BOIUNA This flesh-eating serpent goddess slithers through the Amazon River. Her bright lantern eyes light up the night as she searches for victims. Women get pregnant just being near her.

INTI The Incas called themselves the children of the sun, and their ruler, the Sapa Inca, was a direct descendant of this most important sun god. Gold was Inti's sweat, eclipses were his anger. Widely worshiped, he was usually shown as a disk with a face surrounded by sun's rays. His most important temple was in Cuzco. There the temple walls, the models of garden trees, plants, animals, and even the soil were sheeted in gold. Inside, Inti was represented as a huge plate of solid gold, underneath which were the revered mummies of past Inca rulers.

JAGUAR All kinds of Central and South American sacred artifacts bear fanged images of this deified animal, although there is not a great deal of information about its cults. Shamans used jaguar teeth or bones in their visionary quests. Some myths say an eclipse happens when a sky jaguar eats the sun or moon. Other myths tell of a time when Jaguar was the Master of Fire and the great hunter who gave human beings the bow and arrow, only to see them steal his fire.

KUAT Not only did the vultures have all the world's light, but their broad wingspans blocked the sky. So Kuat, the sun god of Amazon tribal myth, hid himself in a corpse. When the king of the vultures came to eat the maggots, Kuat jumped out of the body and held the bird by the leg until he gave the dark world light.

MANCO CAPAC AND MAMA OCOLLO As king of Cuzco, Manco Capac taught men the agricultural arts, toolmaking, and irrigation. The queen, Mama Ocollo, taught women cooking and weaving. Some Inca myths say they were children of the sun god **Inti,** who told them to found a city wherever they could sink a magic gold rod into the ground. Inner Cuzco formed an outline of a puma.

PACHACAMAC His coastal Peruvian temple was so magnificent, his cult so powerful that even the conquering Incas respected this ancient creator god. He made the first people but forgot to feed them. The first man died; the first woman was starving, so Pachacamac made her pregnant. He chopped up her firstborn son and planted the body parts. Maize and manioc grew from the child's teeth and bones; vegetables sprouted from his flesh. The god's wife, Pachama, was the earth goddess of fertility and creator of animals. Worshipers offered her coca leaves and animal sacrifices, while Pachacamac's temple was an important pilgrimage site. Under Inca rule he became a sun god.

VIRACOCHA He commanded the sun, moon, and stars to rise out of Lake Titicaca. He directed people to emerge from hills, lakes, and caves. He decreed that **Manco Capac** should rule the Incas and that they should be lords of the other Andean peoples. Viracocha was a most powerful creator god, who wore a sun crown and carried thunderbolts. He was a solar and storm deity and possibly an aspect of **Inti.** Viracocha provided the human beings he created from clay with their national languages, dress, and customs and with precious seeds. He wandered among them as a bearded, old white man who preached morality and worked miracles. Then he disappeared—some myths say over the mountain, some say he threw his cloak on the ocean and sailed off on it.

The people created by **Viracocha** emerged from different places in the landscape, which they then held sacred. Throughout South America, there are shrines and *apachitas* (stone piles) at *huacas*, natural sites considered to be holy places endowed with spirits. A *huaca* could be a tree or a mountaintop, a stone relic or a spring, a cave or a burial cairn with mummified bodies. There were many local *huacas*, which people honored with offerings. *Huacas* could also be objects filled with supernatural power.

❧

◄ *Maize was the most important crop throughout the Americas. It was used as food and to make chicha, an intoxicating drink. This pottery stirrup from the Mochica people of northern Peru shows three corn deities. Stirrups were used to hold liquids that the dead would need in the afterlife.*

OCEANIA AND AUSTRALIA

One cannot enumerate the shells of all the things that this world produces.
—TAHITIAN CREATION STORY, POLYNESIA

The mythologies of Oceania and Australia are as deep as the Pacific Ocean that surrounds them. They tell of long, symbolic journeys; creation but no beginning; time that is timeless; gods, heroes, even animals whose actions shaped the world.

All these myths and their fascinating variations were shared orally by kin, clan, or island group. They passed down their myths through the sacred stories, chants, art, and ritual reenactments that were an essential part of their lives. That way of life changed forever when the Europeans arrived, first in the late 16th century and in full force by the 19th century.

Sailing through Oceania

Oceanian myth cannot be neatly summed up by one pantheon, because Oceania itself is three different cultural groups: Polynesia, Melanesia, and Micronesia.

Some of Oceania's most well-known myths come from Polynesia, a great triangle formed by the Hawaiian Islands, Easter Island, and New Zealand. Many other islands, such as Tonga, Samoa, and Tahiti, lie inside the triangle. The Polynesians, especially the Maori of New Zealand, developed a family of gods, although they were called different names on different islands. Stories about Maui, the trickster hero and champion of humankind, are popular and widespread.

Melanesia includes Papua New Guinea, the Fiji islands, and all the southwest Pacific islands in between. Melanesians are incredibly diverse and so are their myths. Most assume that the world has always existed and don't mention a supreme god. Other Melanesian myths tell about the first people and the heroes who taught them how to behave.

Micronesia, the smallest Oceanian group, includes four island archipelagos, the Gilbert, Marshall, Mariana, and Caroline islands. Their myths, which have some traces of Polynesian myths, were often told by poets in great story cycles.

Dreamtime in Australia

For 50,000 years before the Europeans arrived, Australia had been inhabited by Aboriginal peoples. They lived as nomadic hunter-gatherers and developed incredibly complex mythologies. The Aboriginal peoples believe that in an ancient era, or dreamtime, their ancestors walked across Australia giving the continent its natural features, bringing forth all creatures, and establishing order and ritual. Each clan developed its own particular myths about when these creator ancestors passed through the clan's territory. Aboriginal peoples become these ancestors and the present becomes dreamtime during certain sacred ceremonies.

Opposite: Statues, Easter Island, Polynesia

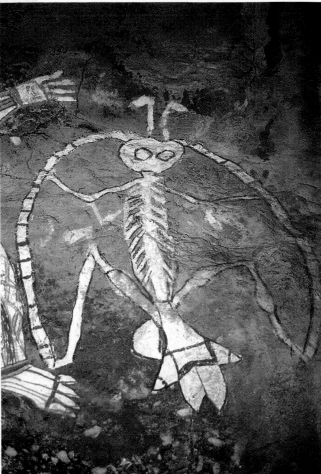

▶ *A rock painting from one of Australia's Aboriginal peoples.*

∽

In the dreamtime, the ancient ancestors of the Aboriginal peoples of Australia crisscrossed the continent. These sky heroes, earth mothers, lizards, snakes, cats, birds, or kangaroos carved out the landscape, created life, named things, and gave people tools like the boomerang or the stone knife. They also showed people how to perform sacred ceremonies and initiation rituals. When they had fulfilled their mission, some of the dreamtime ancestors ascended to the heavens to become constellations; most went to sleep underground or slipped down into waterholes; and the *wandinja* clan spirits turned into rock paintings. Aboriginal peoples carved and painted these events on rocks and bark. They often renew their work during dreamtime ceremonies.

BOBBI-BOBBI To feed the Binbinga of northern Australia, this ancestor snake sent them flying foxes. But the people couldn't catch the bats. Bobbi-Bobbi gave them one of his ribs. The curved bone knocked down the bats and returned to the thrower's hand. It was the first boomerang.

BUE A ray of light shone on a mortal woman, and she gave birth to this Micronesian son of the sun god. Bue snared his golden father with a coconut leaf and made him share his knowledge. Then the hero taught the Gilbert Islanders how to build houses and boats, cure diseases, and sing poetry.

DJANGGAWUL Following the morning star, two divine sisters and their brother paddled away toward northern Australia. They brought sacred objects of the Aboriginal peoples: a womblike mat, a dilly bag for ceremonial objects, and *rangaa* walking sticks. The brother thrust his rangaa into the ground and water gushed out; trees grew where the sisters' sticks touched down. As the women walked the earth, they gave birth to the first humans and pulled others from the mat or dilly bag. The Djanggawul created animals and plants, too. One day while the divine women were fishing, their brother stole their songs and dilly bag. Ever since, men have held all ritualistic power.

HAKAWAU This old Maori sorcerer challenged two evil magicians who kept a magic wooden head, the sight of which knocked anyone dead. As Hakawau neared its spirit house, the head bellowed and flashed deadly beams; the sage just kept walking and chanting. When the head began to moan, the evil sorcerers trembled. Hakawau tossed away the head, clapped his hands once, and the evil duo dropped dead.

HAUMEA "Many bodies had this woman, Haumea," begins a Hawaiian chant. This fertility goddess was continually reborn so she could marry her sons and grandsons to populate the earth. Her magic trees produced any kind of food, including fish, until one day an impatient descendant shook the tree near the ocean and all the fish fell off and swam away.

HINE One of her full names was Hine-titama, the dawn maiden. But when she found out that her husband **Tane** was actually her father, too, Hine fled to the underworld and became the Maori goddess of death, Hine-nui-te-Po. Her staring green eyes appeared to those about to die. **Maui** once tried to cheat death when he caught Hine sleeping. If he could crawl inside her and out of her mouth, he could live forever. The great hero almost succeeded, but a bird laughed at the ridiculous sight. Hine woke up and crushed Maui to death. All people then became mortal.

KAMAPUA'A This popular Hawaiian pig god was mad for love or war and used his huge snout in either adventure. His snorting terrified his enemies, and he followed through with mighty swings from an enormous club. He once rooted down through the earth, chasing some goddesses; his digging created springs. He also pursued **Pele,** but the courtship caused all kinds of natural disasters.

KAMBEL As this Melanesian sky god was walking by a large palm tree, he heard curious sounds and whispers coming from its trunk. He split the tree open, and the first people walked out.

KU AND LONO Ku was the fierce earth god of war; Lono was the peaceful sky god of agriculture. Together they represented an important Hawaiian fertility cult. Lono lived on Earth for four months and brought the rains needed for cultivation. During this time, his statue was carried around the Hawaiian islands to receive gifts and tributes. Then Lono symbolically died and would be reborn eight months later. In between Ku ruled; he required human sacrifice. Other Polynesians called these gods **Tu and Rongo,** the offspring of **Papa and Rangi.**

KUNAPIPI Sometimes the rainbow serpent traveled in front of this old woman as she gave birth to people and called out the animals during dreamtime. Sometimes she was the great snake itself. This fertility and mother goddess of the Aboriginal peoples of northern Australia is celebrated in sacred rituals of initiation.

MAKE-MAKE On Polynesia's remote Easter Island, this creator god protected nesting birds. Every year people watched for the birds. The first man to find an egg became the Bird Man. He shaved off his hair, eyebrows, and eyelashes and lived alone for the next year.

Kane, the remote creator god of Hawaii, created upper and lower heaven and earth and then asked the earth god Ku and the god of heaven, Lono, to help him finish the world. Kane is similar to the other Polynesian deity Tane.

*▼ The ferocious grin on this feather statue of the Hawaiian war god **Ku** is made of polished dog teeth. Members of the Hawaiian nobility often wore feathered helmets.*

▲ *"Illustrious, miraculous, mighty" all are words used in traditional Maori chants that tell of **Maui**'s fishing feat. In this Maori wood carving, Maui is reeling in the large fish that represents New Zealand. His body is decorated with the famous Maori style of tattooing.*

MANGAR-KUNGER-KUNJA

During the dreamtime, this lizard ancestor of the Aranda in central Australia found primeval lumps that were barely human: Their stiff limbs were clamped around their torsos; their eyes, ears, and mouths were shut tight. The lizard cut free the first people and gave them tools, such as the ax and the boomerang. In the northwest, the Karadjeri believed they were created by the Bagadjimbiri, ancestor gods who first appeared as dingo dogs and shaped people partly from mushrooms.

MAUI

When Maui of a Thousand Tricks did not like the ways things were, he changed them. He irked the gods, improved life for mortals, and became the most popular Polynesian hero. Maui thought there wasn't enough time between sunrise and sunset. People didn't have enough light to work, cook, or make bark cloth. So Maui lassoed the sun and beat the sun god with his grandmother's magic jawbone until the golden one agreed to move more slowly across the sky. The sky itself bothered Maui. It was too low, so he shoved it up higher. He turned his brother-in-law into a dog, the first domesticated animal, and tricked an underworld ancestor into pulling out almost all of her flaming fingernails so he could bring fire to Earth. Maui's greatest adventure was on a fishing trip with his brothers. They wouldn't share their bait, so Maui punched his own nose and used his blood to fish. He hauled in catches so big they became the Polynesian islands.

NAREAU

Some Micronesians used this name for two creator gods: an elder spider god and his trickster grandson. The elder spider existed alone at the beginning of time, but he soon created other beings and charged them with creating the world. One, the eel god Riiki, stretched up to separate the earth and sky. Another, the octopus god Na Kika, spread his eight arms, gathering sand and stones to make islands. A third, the younger Nareau, slew his father and used his eyes for the sun and moon, bits of his brain for the stars, and his flesh and bones for rocks and stones. Then Nareau made humans.

OLOFAT This Micronesian trickster god was half mortal, half divine. He could run as soon as he was born and shortly after climbed a column of smoke up to heaven, looking for his sky relatives. They weren't all glad to see him, so Olofat stirred up trouble. He gave sharks their teeth and stingrays their poison sting. Then he faked his death at the hands of some gods, only to terrorize them with his "resurrection." Olofat also played tricks on humans, but did bring them fire and served as their messenger to the gods.

PAPA AND RANGI The Polynesian mother earth goddess and father sky god were locked in a such a passionate embrace that none of their children could be born. Their children were divided over what to do: **Tawhiri-ma-tea** wanted to leave them be; **Tane** and Rongo wanted to separate them; **Tu** wanted to kill them. Papa and Rangi's eternal sadness at separating created mist and dew. Meanwhile, their children kept feuding.

PELE This tempestuous Hawaiian fire goddess once left her home in the Kilauea volcano. At a hula dance she fell in love with a young chief, Lohiau. Before returning to her crater, she promised to marry the mortal. Pele sent her sister to get Lohiau, but the chief died of a broken heart before she arrived.

The sister restored him to life and fell in love with him, too. Pele was furious and belched out red-hot lava flows, killing them both. In another of her fiery fits, the volcano goddess erupted when the pig god Kamapua'a doused Pele with rain and fog and set hogs loose all over her lands. Other gods had to intervene so that the world's fire would not be lost in a deluge.

QAT He wasn't divine, he wasn't mortal, he wasn't even really born. This Melanesian trickster spirit burst out of a rock. After he made rocks, trees, and pigs, Qat carved people out of wood. He danced and drummed around his figures until they came to life. Unfortunately, his spider sidekick, Marawa, copied him. But the spider buried his people in a pit, and they rotted. And so death was brought into the world.

▶ A malanggan *memorial figure from Northern New Ireland.*

All Oceanian peoples believed that a person's spirit survived death, and ancestor worship was very widespread. The Melanesians on New Ireland had elaborate death rituals, which included carving memorial *malanggans* (left). In many Oceanic stories, death came about because of a mistake or foolishness, as in the Polynesian myth about **Maui** and **Hine** or the Melanesian myth about **Qat** and Marawa. According to an Aboriginal people, the Worora, life was self-renewing until the black python berated her dead husband for returning after she had already shaved her head and put on mourning ashes. He went back to his grave, and ever since people have had to die. Some Melanesian islanders believed dead people shed their skins like snakes and became reborn. But once a crying child did not recognize her reborn mother. The woman then put on her old familiar skin, which never came off again. After that, people were no longer rejuvenated but died.

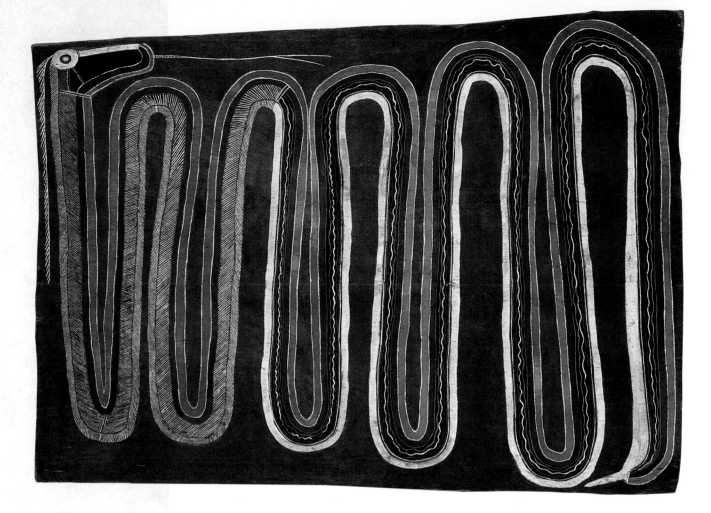

▲ Many Australian Aboriginal bark paintings, like this 20th-century example, depict the rainbow serpent. Different Aboriginal peoples call this serpent by different names, such as **Kunapipi** or **Yurlungur.**

TA'AROA "He has always been. . . . He is within. He is the form," says a Tahitian hymn in praise of this creator god. Ta'aroa dwelt in dark silence in the primeval egg. He finally pushed himself out, only to find that the egg was all that existed. The god used part of the shell to make the sky and part to make the earth. In some myths, he then built his own temple from his body; in others he used his body parts to form clouds, mountains, trees, and fish.

TANE The Maori forest god grew like a tree, pushing his trunk down on the earth, pressing his branches up to the heavens to separate his parents **Papa and Rangi.** Tane mated with other beings and produced streams, stones, animals, and grass—but nothing like himself. So the forest god built a woman in the sand and breathed life into her. She became his wife and the mother of **Hine.**

TANGAROA As Maori god of the sea, he was most unhappy when some of his creatures fled **Tawhiri-ma-tea**'s tempest and moved onto the land. His brother **Tane,** god of the forest, felt the same way when he saw fish, originally forest-dwellers, wriggle into the sea. The two siblings have squabbled ever since. Tangaroa sends waves crashing to the shore, eating away at the land. Tane lets people use his trees and plants to build canoes and fishnets to conquer the seas.

TAWHIRI-MA-TEA The Maori god of windstorms was furious at his siblings for separating their parents, **Papa and Rangi.** He whipped the seas into a frenzy with his wild winds and toppled whole forests with his hurricanes. This not only caused a terrible flood but set his brothers **Tane** and **Tangaroa** against each other. Only **Tu** was powerful enough to defeat Tawhiri-ma-tea, who still plagues Polynesian islanders with his violent outbursts.

TU The Maori war god's full name is Tu-mataugena. After their parents, **Papa and Rangi,** were forced apart, Tu tried to put a stop to his brother **Tawhiri-ma-tea**'s blustery rampaging. The struggle between the two of them helped gouge out the Pacific Ocean. Tu did not appreciate having to face the wrath of his brother alone, so he took revenge on his other siblings. He ate their offspring, trapped their animals, netted their fish, and uprooted their plants. He is the fierce patron of warriors.

WANDJINA Every Aboriginal clan of Australia is protected by one of these ancestor spirits, also associated with fertility and rain. The spirits painted their own images on rocks so that people could have access to their power. The haloed *wandjina* have no mouths; if they did, it would always be raining.

WAWALAG SISTERS They walked through Australia's Arnhem lands, naming many places, plants, and animals. When they stopped at a sacred water hole, one sister gave birth, and the other tried to cook. Some blood seeped into the water hole. Then the food plants and animals jumped right out of the pot and leaped into the pool. Lightning flashed and thunder crashed. The sisters chanted, fearing they had disturbed the water hole's serpent. They had. **Yurlungur** lulled them to sleep with his singing and then swallowed them and their babies. A devastating flood followed. Then, in some myths, the python vomited up the women and children. In others, the sisters are being punished for sleeping with men from a forbidden clan.

YURLUNGUR He arched across the sky as a rainbow. He slithered across Australia shaping the landscape, scooping out waterways. Yulungur is one of the rainbow serpent's many names. Feared and revered by Aboriginal peoples, this creature could stand straight up or stretch across miles and miles of country while still keeping his tail in his sacred water hole. Yurlungur was usually coiled deep in his sacred pool at Mirrimina, whose water shimmered with rainbow colors. When disturbed by the **Wawalag Sisters,** the huge copper python ate them.

One of Australia's most famous sites is a huge, red rock that rises straight up out of the desert sand. This sandstone monolith soars 1,100 feet high and is about five miles around. Its traditional owners, the Anangut, call it Uluru or "the meeting place." They consider the rock a very sacred site and hold initiation and other secret ceremonies there. The Anangut interpret markings on the rocks as signs of their ancestors' presence and consider Uluru the home of many mythic beings. Uluru is called Ayers Rock by English speakers.

❧

SELECTED BIBLIOGRAPHY

These books are rich sources of information and visuals. The titles with asterisks (*) are particularly good for children and young adults. The titles in **boldface** are retellings of myths.

Series
* **Looking at Myths and Legends.** NTC Publishing Group
* **Myths and Legends of the World.** Margaret McElderry Books
* **Oxford Myths and Legends.** Oxford University Press
* **The World Mythology Series.** Peter Bedrick Books

General
Bonheim, Jalaja (ed.). *Goddess: A Celebration in Art and Literature.* Stewart, Tabori and Chang. 1997

A Dictionary of World Mythology. G. P. Putnam's Sons. 1980

Cavendish, Richard (ed.). *Mythology: An Illustrated Encyclopedia.* Barnes and Noble, Inc. 1992

Cotterell, Arthur. *The Macmillan Illustrated Encyclopedia of Myths and Legends.* Macmillan. 1989

Eliot, Alexander. *The Universal Myths.* NAL/Penguin Books. 1990

Grimal, Pierre (ed.). *Larousse World Mythology.* Excalibur Books, Simon and Schuster. 1981

*Hamilton, Virginia. **In the Beginning: Creation Stories from Around the World.** Harcourt Brace. 1988.

*Langley, Myrtle. *Religion.* Dorling Kindersley. 1996

*McCaughrean, Geraldine. **The Bronze Cauldron.** Margaret McElderry Books. 1999

The Crystal Pool. McElderry. 1998

The Golden Hoard. McElderry. 1997

The Silver Treasure. McElderry. 1997

Oliphant, Margaret. *The Atlas of the Ancient World: Charting the Great Civilizations of the Past.* Simon and Schuster. 1992

*Osborne, Mary Pope. *One World, Many Religions.* Alfred A. Knopf, Inc. 1996

*Philip, Neil. **The Illustrated Book of Myths.** Dorling Kindersley. 1995

Smith, Huston. *The World's Religions.* HarperCollins. 1991

Willis, Roy (gen. ed.). *World Mythology.* Henry Holt and Company, New York. 1993

India
*Dalal-Clayton, Diksha; Heeger, Marilyn. **The Adventures of Young Krishna: The Blue God of India.** Oxford University Press. 1997

Ions, Veronica. *Indian Mythology.* Paul Hamlyn Ltd. 1967

*Katz, Brian P. *Deities and Demons of the Far East.* MetroBooks. 1995

Narayan, R.K. **Gods, Demons, and Others.** Viking Press. 1964

O'Flaherty, Wendy (intro.). *Hindu Myths.* Penguin. 1975

*Wangu, Madhu Bazaz. *Hinduism.* Facts on File, Inc. 1991

China
* Birch, Cyril. **Chinese Myths and Legends.** Oxford University Press. 1993

*Sanders, Tao Tao Liu. **Dragons, Gods, and Spirits from Chinese Mythology.** Peter Bedrick Books. 1980

Yuan Ke. *Dragons and Dynasties: An Introduction to Chinese Mythology.* Penguin Group. 1993

Japan
*McAlpine, Helen and William. **Japanese Tales and Legends.** Oxford University Press. 1958

Piggott, Juliet. *Japanese Mythology.* Hamlyn Publishing Group. 1969

Southeast Asia
*Spagnoli, Cathy. **Asian Tales and Tellers.** August House Publishers. 1998

*Sun, Ruth Q. *Land of Seagull and Fox.* John Weatherhill, Inc. 1966

Africa
Knappert, Jan. *African Mythology.* Diamond Books. 1990

*Mbitu, Ngangar and Prime, Ranchor. **Essential African Mythology.** HarperCollins. 1997

Radin, Paul (ed.). **African Folktales.** Schocken Books. 1983

*Zona, Guy T. *The House of the Heart Is Never Full and other Proverbs of Africa.* Simon and Schuster. 1993

Egypt
Ames, Delano. *Egyptian Mythology.* Paul Hamlyn Ltd. 1965

Barrett, Clive. *The Egyptian Gods and Goddesses.* Diamond Books. 1996

*Harris, Geraldine. **Gods and Pharaohs from Egyptian Mythology.** Peter Bedrick Books. 1991

The Near East
Hinnells, John R. *Persian Mythology*. Hamlyn Publishing Group. 1973
Knappert, Jan. *Middle Eastern Mythology and Religion*. Element Books. 1993
*Matthews, Andrews. **Markduk the Mighty and Other Stories of Creation.** Millbrook Press. 1997
McCall, Henrietta. *Mesopotamian Myths*. British Museum Press/University of Austin Press. 1990

Greece
Boardman, John; Griffin, Jasper; Murray, Oswyn. *Greece and the Hellenistic World*. Oxford University Press. 1994
*Bulfinch, Thomas. **The Illustrated Age of Fable.** Stewart, Tabori, and Chang. 1998
*Bulfinch, Thomas; Holme, Bryan (comp.); Campbell, Joseph (intro.). **Myths of Greece and Rome.** Penguin Books. 1981
*D'Aulaire, Edgar and Ingri. **D'Aulaire's Book of Greek Myths.** Doubleday. 1962
Fagles, Robert (trans.). *The Odyssey*. Penguin/Putnam. 1996
Graves, Robert. *The Greek Myths* (Vols. 1 and 2). Penguin Books. 1960
Lattimore, Richmond (trans.). *The Iliad of Homer*. University of Chicago Press. 1951
*Osborne, Mary Pope. **Favorite Greek Myths.** Scholastic, Inc. 1991

Rome
*Gifford, Douglas. **Heroes, Gods, and Emperors.** Peter Bedrick Books. 1993
Fitzgerald, Robert (trans.). *The Aeneid*. Vintage Books, Random House. 1983
Perowne, Stewart. *Roman Mythology*. Hamlyn Publishing Group. 1969

Celtic Lands
*Clark, Lindsay. **Essential Celtic Mythology.** HarperCollins, London. 1997
Coghlan, Ronan. *The Illustrated Encyclopedia of Arthurian Legend*. Element Books. 1993
Cotterell, Arthur. *Celtic Mythology*. Smithmark Publishers. 1997
*Ellis, Peter Berrisford. **The Chronicles of the Celts.** Carroll and Graf. 1999
MacKillop, James. *Dictionary of Celtic Mythology*. Oxford University Press. 1998

Norse Lands
*Branston, Brian. **Gods and Heroes from Viking Mythology.** Peter Bedrick Books. 1994

Davidson, H.R. Ellis. *Scandinavian Mythology*. Peter Bedrick Books. 1986
*Osborne, Mary Pope. **Favorite Norse Myths.** Scholastic, Inc. 1996
Sturluson, Snorri; Jean I. Young. *The Prose Edda*. University of California Press. 1954

North America
*Bruchac, Joseph. **Four Ancestors: Stories, Songs, and Poems from Native North America.** Bridgewater Books. 1996
Flying with the Eagle, Racing the Great Bear. Bridgewater Books. 1995
The Girl Who Married the Moon. Bridgewater Books. 1996
Burland, Cottie. *North American Indian Mythology*. Barnes and Noble, Inc. 1985
Gill, Sam; Sullivan, Irene. *Dictionary of Native American Mythology*. Oxford University Press. 1994
Mayo, Gretchen. **Earthmaker's Tales.** Walker. 1989
Star Tales. Walker. 1987
Taylor, Colin F. *Native American Myths and Legends*. Smithmark Publishers, Inc. 1994

Central America
Nicholson, Irene. *Mexican and Central American Mythology*. Paul Hamlyn Ltd. 1967
*Sexton, James D. **Mayan Folktales.** University of New Mexico Press. 1999
Taube, Karl. *Aztec and Maya Myths*. British Museum Press/University of Austin Press. 1993

South America
Osborne, Harold. *South American Mythology*. Peter Bedrick Books. 1988
Urton, Gary. *Inca Myths*. British Museum Press/University of Austin Press. 1999

Oceania and Australia
Knappert, Jan. *Pacific Mythology*. Diamond Books. 1995
*Oodgeroo. **Dreamtime: Aboriginal Stories.** Lothrop, Lee and Shepard Books. 1972
Poignant, Rosalyn. *Oceanic Mythology*. Hamlyn Publishing Group. 1967
*Thompson, Vivian; Kahalewai, Marilyn. **Hawaiian Myths of Earth, Sea, and Sky.** University of Hawaii Press. 1988

Electronic
Encyclopedia Mythica http://www.pantheon.org/mythica
The Perseus Project http://www.perseus.tufts.edu
(Gregory R. Crane, ed.; Tufts University/Yale University/ The National Endowment for the Humanities)

Index